alabado
A Story of Old California

alabado
A Story of Old California

by

Paul H. Kocher

FRANCISCAN HERALD PRESS
1434 WEST 51st STREET • CHICAGO, 60609

Library of Congress Cataloging in Publication Data

Kocher, Paul H
  Alabado.

  1. California—History—To 1846. 2. Indians of
North America—California—Missions. 3. Missions—
California. I. Title.
F864.K6   979.4802   77-26203
ISBN 0-8199-0689-1

ALABADO Y EN SALZADO SEA
Praised and worshiped be

EL DIVINO SACRAMENTO, EN QUIEN DIOS
The Divine Sacrament, in which God,

OCULTO ASISTE DE LAS ALMAS EL SUSTENTO.
Hidden, helps to nourish souls.

Y LA LIMPIE CONCEPCION
And praised be the Immaculate Conception

DE LA REYNA DE LOS CIELOS
Of Mary, Queen of Heaven,

QUE QUEDANDO VIRGEN PURA
Who, remaining a pure Virgin,

ES MADRE DEL VERBO ETERNO.
Is the Mother of the eternal Word.

Y EL BENEDITO SAN JOSÉ
Praised, too, be the Blessed Saint Joseph,

ELECTO POR DIOS IMMENSO
Chosen by God Almighty

PARA PADRE ESTIMATIVO
As worthy to be the foster father

DE SU HIJO EL DIVINO VERBO.
Of His Son, the Divine Word.

ESTO ES POR TODOS LOS SIGLOS,
This Son is for all the ages to come

Y DE LOS SIGLOS AMEN
And from all the ages past. Amen.

AMEN JESUS Y MARIA
Amen, Jesus and Mary,

JESUS MARIA Y JOSÉ!
Jesus, Mary, and Joseph!

Chapter 1

When the chia-seed baskets were almost empty, the
strips of dried venison almost all eaten, and spring in
full bloom at last, Chinichinic, war chief of the Chumash tribe, which bore his name, sent out the hunting
and fishing parties in all directions, as custom and
necessity required. Also, according to custom, each
party was small but wellrounded, its members having
diverse skills. That led by Temi, the ceremonial chief,
for instance, consisted of only four families besides his
own, but among the heads of these families, Cayatu
and Muniyaut knew how to hunt the land while
Thaas and Sesecl seldom failed to gather a rich harvest
from the sea in the latter's plank canoe.

Temi had not come this time to join in the sacred
chase, though he rated as a good hunter. He knew he
would soon be called upon to display his dancing
before the pale strangers who were expected to visit
his tribe. With the dances he had newly invented, and
still needed to rehearse, he intended to show them
what a Chumash ceremonial chief could do in both
his serious and his comic roles.

During the hunting, Temi reflected, the hunters
would bring in the kill from land and sea. The women
would smoke the flesh, cut it into long strips, and
soften the hides of the warm-blooded mammals. The
girls would help them. And the older boys, with their
light harpoons and their half-strength bows, would
get ready to be men.

1

All except his own son, Ixtil. Temi needed the youngster to play his flutes and whistles while he danced. He was not at all sure that he liked the boy to be spending so many hours with the tribe's shaman, Werowance, who had inserted himself so cleverly into the party at the last moment. Would the boy want to become another Werowance? He'd see about that when he had time, after practicing the new dance.

Temi need not have worried. Ixtil, at the age of fourteen, still retained in full the faculty of wonder he had had since he first learned to toddle from one astonishing place to another. His reason for sitting often with the old shaman was simply that the wizard talked with him, man to man, as nobody else did.

Besides, Werowance knew the answers to many questions about things and people, particularly about the spirits which people turned into when their bodies went cold and had to be buried. Then they somehow became connected with a mysterious male god, Sup, or with his wife Achup, who stood for all things female. Together, they had made all living creatures, but for some reason they did not like to be troubled with petitions, or even to be mentioned often, and then only in a particular tone called "reverence." Every person, animal, and even place had a voice of its own which must be listened for and answered properly.

Often, after repeating this warning, the shaman would break off abruptly, leaving Ixtil more confused. Wondering, the lad would watch the old man retire inside his hut, specially built for him by the men of the hunting party before they built the five others along the streamside to house their own families.

Ixtil, however, did not really mind being suddenly abandoned. No day had enough hours in it to give him time for all the things he wanted to do, and all

of them simultaneously. He loved to help Sesecl and
Thaas caulk the leaks in Sesecl's canoe with bitumen.
Always, the sea looked for ways to come in where
the planks fitted together. The owners of canoes never
failed to bring with them, even on short journeys, a
big lump of tar which they traded for, way down the
coast, with another Chumash tribe that owned pits
where the earth bubbled it out. Ixtil had learned how
to heat the lump over the special fire which Sesecl
kept going and to carry it quickly to him in an abalone
shell. If the lump should be used up, Ixtil took pride
in the knowledge that he could usually find some small
dabs of the tar on the beach where the stream flowed
into the sea. If unlucky at that, he could always run
to a place where the tribe had found the sticky black
stuff oozing slowly out from under a rock. But that
was far.

In return, Sesecl and Thaas sometimes took Ixtil
fishing with them. Oh, the joy of launching the canoe
through the surf at just the right moment, the swift,
bouncing ride while paddles flashed, and of helping
the two experts throw out with a swish the wide,
closely meshed net! Then, without entanglement, dropping his own handline with its baited abalone hook,
the sudden tug, the breathless pulling in to see what
he had caught! And then his shout if a gleaming
albacore flopped inside, big enough to satisfy his
whole family that night!

"We are the sea people," Sesecl would tell him
proudly. "We live near it. It feeds us well."

Ixtil decided that he would build the finest canoe
anyone had ever seen, when he finished growing up.

One noon he lay dreaming under the sycamore which
spread its shade over the stream's border quite near
the camp, thinking how splended his canoe would be.
He would call it *Wave Witch,* perhaps. But as was

usual with him, dreaming quickly grew stale.

He spooted a mockingbird reciting its interwoven borrowings from the sycamore's highest tip and glimpsed a yellow flicker dart across the water. That reminded him of his promise to his mother to bring her some bright new feathers for the dress she wore when the women danced. His father could use some, too, in the long ceremonial robe, which came down to his ankles.

Jumping to his feet, he ran to the hut for his small bird-bow and a handful of arrows of various sizes. To the half-strength hunting bow appropriate to his age, however, he gave only a look of scorn. Once in the woods, he drew from its hiding place in a hollow oak the much larger and stiffer man's bow he had secretly made. After all, a hunter could never tell what he might need when hunting alone. At least a rabbit or two, perhaps a buck, possibly even a wildcat. But not a grizzly bear, Lord Sup—especially not one with cubs! Ixtil knew he could not outrun a bear, as most of the adult hunters could. Sup would certainly notice that he was out only for birds, and would, please, keep away bears with cubs, of which there were altogether too many in this area these days.

Quiet stalking brought Ixtil close enough to give him killing shots at several blackbirds with crimson-shouldered wings, a robin, a thrush, some yellow banded cedar-waxwings, and a little greenish bird whose name he did not know. His game bag began to fill. He crippled a red-tailed hawk, but had to chase its flutterings before he could add its plumage to his catch. Also, great luck was his, or Sup's help, when he brought down several brilliant hummingbirds, blurring as they fed at a flowering honeysuckle.

He might well turn back now, he thought. With the white feathers he could get later from the gulls in the bay and the gray ones from a sandpiper or two, twinkling their little feet after every wave, he could perhaps please his mother into making for him one of her necklaces from the round cores of clam shells. He'd then be one up on his rival and friend Sioctu, son of the war chief, whose necklace had many crudely shaped cores.

Ixtil stopped still to enjoy the daydream. In the quiet, he suddenly heard, then saw, a doe and her fawn step daintily into the clearing ahead. At once he strung his man's bow and set a long, sharply tipped arrow to its cord of sinew. But he did not let it fly. Shooting the fawn was beneath him, and if he slew its mother the fawn would surely die, too. The tribe was not so hungry as that. He must wait for the buck, if there was one.

A shaking of the underbrush to his right drew his eyes and gave them one quick sight of antlers. What a triumph if he could walk into camp with that one slung over his shoulders! It was well that so often he had secretly sent pieces of bark bobbing down the river and so often hit them with his arrows. Nibbling on, unaware, the buck moved slightly, giving Ixtil for one brief moment a clearer view. The bow twanged and the arrow pierced the living throat. Blood spurted, crimsoning the whole neck. After a few frantic leaps the buck fell. Quickly, Ixtil knelt over it and stabbed his keen obsidian knife deeper into the wound.

Though the buck outweighed Ixtil, he manged to walk into camp erect, nonchalant, carrying its heavy body on his back. Of course he gave no sign, except a grin, on hearing the cheers and questions of the hunting party. But his mother, Maya, knew that this was only the third deer he had ever killed and that he lacked experience in butchering it.

She led the way downstream, well out of sight of

the village, Ixtil following her at a distance. She reminded him how to use his knife to free the skin from the carcass and to carve the meat underneath into thin strips to be smoked and dried. What could not be easily preserved in this way—the heart, liver, kidneys, stomach, and intestines—if judiciously distributed, would feed everyone in camp as an evening meal. With the compliments of Ixtil!

He gave the precious skin to his mother, which she would work patiently into a new skirt. It would cover her modestly front and back and hang warmly halfway down her legs. Ixtil could visualize her in the skirt. Of course, above the waist she would wear a cape of soft otter skins, rare in the camp; there was nothing better for cold weather and ceremonial occasions. All this in addition to the feather dress he was preparing for her.

Maya got to work on the deerskin, scraping it clean with a sharp flint to make it ready for tanning. But Ixtil soon lost interest in the endless scraping, which belonged to women and so could never be any concern of his.

Jubilantly, he ran to the beach and plunged into the sea, just as if he were his father cooling off after a long sweat in the half-underground *temescal,* the sweathouse, which is heated inside by a big fire. The sea was very calm and clear, and he swam about for a while. Then, emptying his lungs of air, he sank to the sandy bottom, where he lay unstirring, looking up at the surface a half dozen feet above him. Between it and his eyes many fish swam by: several large cod and mackerel, schools of fingerlings keeping close together, a rare small salmon, and even an otter, all weirdly distorted in size and shape as clouds passed across the sun, bringing alternate shadow and light to the water.

Suddenly a sea lion loomed like a monster, and Ixtil scrambled ashore. Not that he was afraid of mere sea lions, once he stood safely on land, but what had he feared while he was in the water? Well, there were two different sea lions, different yet the same. One was a shadowy monster, the other a friendly beast, always watching the strange doings of people on shore. Which one was the real sea lion, he wondered idly, the one he saw through water or the one he saw through air from land?

But his wonderment was brief. He still had to get the feathers from the gulls and sandpipers and, he now added, the red-eyed grebes riding just beyond them, where the waves crested and broke.

By the time Ixtil had filled his game bag with plumes from these birds, the sun was falling into the ocean. Watching it, he wondered how its fire could enter so much water without being quenched, like any other fire. He liked the apple-green of the western sky after the sun had disappeared, and stood for a time admiring it. He trotted back to camp in the dusk, and was not surprised to find that the evening meal, his deer, had already been eaten. But Maya had saved him a juicy piece of liver, sprinkled with seeds she had crushed.

Even in late spring, the nights grew cold. Sitting close to the cooking fire, which crackled in the center of the hut and sent its smoke through the smokehole in the roof directly overhead, Ixtil shivered and remembered that he had been quite naked ever since his swim. His father, across the fire from him, wearing only a loin cover, did not seem to mind. Sister Erlinqua and brother Tecocco, however, both older than he, were wearing short capes of rabbit skins around their shoulders. Maya now draped one around her shoulders, too. For modesty, both she and Erlinqua wore deerskin skirts.

Ixtil, glad that he was not female, asked Temi whether he would be needed at the ceremonial dance rehearsal tomorrow. His father nodded. Then Ixtil lay down on his grass mat, after putting on a cape, and was soon asleep.

Next morning, after food, Ixtil made a small bundle of his flutes and whistles while Temi collected his paints and carefully folded his long coat of many-colored feathers over one arm. This would drape him from shoulder to ankle.

Far from prying eyes, at the remote forest glade which Temi had chosen for his rehearsal, Ixtil watched admiringly while his father costumed himself for the serious speech and action. Some ceremonial chiefs, he knew, when they gave a harangue of welcome to honored guests, laid on the paint in circles of varying hue around legs, arms, and torso. They painted a fixed mask on their face with the expression they wished.

Not Temi. His coat of feathers covered his entire body, and shimmered and rustled as he moved. Feathers, stuck in his hair, formed an aureole. The mask, painted on his face, was not intended to be fixed in any one expression. He could quickly change it by washing off a few lines and replacing them with others.

Temi began by standing statuesquely on the stump of a fallen tree and looking around as if at a huge crowd. As soon as he began his speech of welcome, Ixtil accompanied him softly with a solemn tune on his flute, made from elderwood, the tree of music. Its mellow notes kept time with the sonorous roll of the chief's language. Springing down from the tree stump, Temi, still speaking, moved around the entire glade with stately steps and gestures. Ixtil varied the rhythms of his music accordingly. The official dance and speech of greeting ended at the stump where they had begun.

Then Temi plunged his face into the nearby spring, rubbed out its lines of paint, and quickly substituted others. Ixtil could not help gasping at the change. A grotesque mocking stranger, not his father, leered down at him with rolling eyes. Automatically, he reached for his whistle, the tibia of a deer pierced with holes. Its first notes screeched high, deafeningly. As it parodied the flute, Temi's comic dance parodied the serious dance he had just performed. He howled, he pranced, he shambled, he uttered giberish. His movements became erratic and erotic. They began as if going somewhere, but abruptly stopped and started someshere else.

All was madness, without visible order or completion. As Temi gabbled on, one of his hands, then both, seized his tongue to keep it quiet, but could not. His hands straining in pretense, he walked several times around the glade, making a grunting gobble. It was, to Ixtil, a frightening, masterly role, much better in its way than Temi's stately dance of welcome. Not that he could laugh at it, exactly, but when he grew up no doubt he would, as did the other men of the tribe.

Back at the camp, Ixtil helped his mother by bringing firewood for their hut and for the long line of thin deer-meat slices she was smoking and drying outside. Making flour by grinding seeds with a pestle was a tiresome chore, but he was repaying Maya for helping him with skinning the buck; so he didn't walk off. Also, water had to be carried from the river in the leakproof baskets she had made. Before Ixtil knew it, he was eating supper with his family in their hut. Temi had gone back to being an ordinary mortal again, he noticed with relief.

Another sleep, another awakening, another day. There were so many things for Ixtil to do that, at first, he did none of them. But the memory that came back most often was of Werowance, painting his pictures on a smooth rock wall about a twenty-minute run upstream.

When Ixtil got there, he found the old shaman perched on a rocky ledge above the river's flood mark, painting with red cinnabar pigment. In small pots, within reach of his arm, Werowance also had black and white, but no yellow. Ixtil had brought with him, as a friendship offering, lumps of yellow he had found in a hillside vein on one of his explorations, as well as fragments of charcoal and chalk. Silently, he placed all of them beside the pigments on the ledge. The wizard grunted his acceptance.

Ixtil sat, dangling his legs over the edge, until Werowance would be willing to talk. Meantime he watched the skill of the artist and wondered what the figures he was painting meant. Some of them vaguely resembled men or animals, each with four limbs, and four or five fingers (or whatever they were), on each limb. One which looked like a frog, had a long tail— unlike any frog he had ever seen. Rosettes, triangles, and other geometrical designs, as well as a sun shooting out rays, also were painted on the rock, but in smaller numbers. A canoe on painted wheels seemed to be rolling by.

Werowance sat down to rest beside Ixtil.

"What are they, elder?" the boy asked the old man.

"You ask that again, how many times, Ixtil?" the shaman questioned.

Smiling in answer, Ixtil held up the fingers of both his hands and the toe of one foot.

"Good!" exclaimed the wizard. "Now you are ready to hear a story. Long ago I learned from my grandfather, and he from his, that Hualtepec, a good god, made everything. You understand? *Everything!* You, me, all men and women, animals, plants, fishes, birds, *everything.* But by and by Hualtepec went away to create more worlds, and left Sup to rule this one. But Sup is evil. He runs the world wrong. This makes it bad for us, especially when we die.''

"Die?'' Ixtil asked, afraid. "Why when we die?''

"Because then we become spirits. Now the spirits want to fly out of this evil world to find the good Hualtepec, but Sup does not wish it. He lives up there in the blue sky all around the earth. He throws the spirits back down, and tries to make them do bad things to us, like driving away our food so we starve, or sending an envious tribe to fight us, or thinking up new diseases so we die. *Ai! Ai!* To live our lives in an evil world is not easy. Not even in death can we be free.''

"*Ai! Ai!*'' exclaimed Ixtil, deeply moved. "But can't the spirits slip by Sup when he's not looking?''

The shaman nodded sadly. "But that happens seldom, for Sup to be looking away. So we must try to deceive him. I saw you the other day, lying on the sea's floor and looking up through the water, and the fishes swam over you. How did they look?''

"Disfigured, misty, not like themselves, Werowance.''

"Now look up at the clouds from where we sit. How do they seem through this sea of blue air that lies between them and you?''

"Always moving and changing. Disfigured, misty...''

"And not like themselves,'' prompted Werowance.

"I see,'' said Ixtil slowly. "The clouds are the spirits, changing shape to deceive the eye of Sup until they can slip past him.''

"And how can our paintings help them, perhaps?''

Ixtil shouted exultantly: "By attracting the gaze of the evil god and giving the cloudy spirits a chance to escape! That's how, isn't it?''

The painter nodded. "Add one thing more, boy.

We offer Sup a whole unreal world here, which he thinks is real. Our paintings of men who have died are deformed—just enough so that they will look like the spirits of the men themselves seen through the disfugurement of blue air. For the spirit resembles the body it leaves."

"Let me paint, Sir!" Ixtil cried eagerly. "I will spend all my days painting to free the spirits."

Werowance demurred. "You are too young to decide on an occupation. Take some years. First, learn to paint well. See, this is how you begin."

With charcoal, he outlined a form somewhat like a salamander but with a suggestion of a human face, oddly like that of Kmapse, who had died just before Ixtil's hunting party left the main camp.

Next, the shaman took from his waistband a phial of resin and poured a few drops on the powdered yellow ochre, then mixed them well. He applied this mixture to the side of a rock face with a forefinger, talking as he painted.

"Instead of the creature's front paws, you put hands, but each with only four fingers. And instead of the back paws, legs with the same number of toes. These will help to confuse Sup if he looks in this direction. Now add a tail like a snake. Make the reptilian eyes human by rounding them and giving them lids. But keep the snout, and make it red."

He stepped back to look at the figure. He approved his work, it seemed to Ixtil, for his grim face smiled a little. Standing proudly, the shaman spoke with reverence: "Hualtepec, great and good, make Sup look here for a long time so that the spirit of Kmapse may come to you! Let it be so!"

Then the wizard looked at his young student and said, "Paint!" Ixtil painted on a separate area of rock until midafternoon, but he could approve none of what he did. Neither could Werowance, who scrubbed it off.

"Not bad, but not good. You will have to do this to your painting many times. Sup is not so easily cheated. Tomorrow we must look in the woods together for a new supply of pigments. Eat early."

All the next day they searched through the woods, particularly on barren cliffs and hillsides. Ixtil knew where the yellow waited, but the other hues were so hard to find that they wandered far before filling their pouches. On their way back to camp, Ixtil resolved aloud to mark prominently, from now on, the outcroppings of every vein of color-bearing earth and rock whenever he walked the forest paths.

"That is the right way," agreed his teacher. "If we were at Tixlini, or any of our other main camps, I could easily show you where every color is. But this country is strange to me."

Events the next day, however, drove all thoughts of pointing out of Ixtil's mind. Well before midday, the lookout cried out that Tequie's canoe, rowed by four warriors from the main camp, was approaching. Everybody in camp ran to the shore to watch and shout comments.

Obviously, the canoemen were in a great hurry. Scarcely had the boat's prow touched sand when Tequie himself jumped into the water and raced up the beach to the waiting people.

"The Spaniards are arriving at Tixlini!" he cried. "Chinichinic wants you all there at once."

"'At once' has already passed," said Temi wryly, "but 'soon' has not. We'll be there 'soon,' especially if Tequie will take half our party in his canoe, and part of the food we've gathered."

Each member of the hunting party had spent a good part of his life making and breaking camp and could do his allotted task virtually in his sleep. Before long, people and the fruits of the hunting had been fairly distributed between the two canoes, which the paddlers sent racing over the wavelets of the sunlit sea. The huts of the hunters were left intact for next time.

Chapter 2

Tixlini was so suitable a campsite for the several hundred people of Ixtil's tribe that they had made it their permanent home, winter and summer, for many generations. It lay at the junction of three rivers which wandered lazily through tree-lined banks and across fertile meadows, never quite dry even in the driest summer.

Near the Chumash camp, two large peaks rose unexpectedly from the plain, neither mountains nor hills, exactly, but like the humps of some ancient beast rearing up from underground. The real mountains stretched north and south range after range, some miles east of the plain. About ten miles to the west lay the ocean, from which a restless wind blew morning fogs and, in the winter, rains to refresh Tixlini valley.

Temi's party arrived late in the afternoon, to find a dozen Spaniards sitting round a great fire, talking and smoking together, while the people of Chinichinic's tribe stood back, waiting for their ceremonial chief to greet the strangers properly. Temi quickly donned his long robe of feathers, so painstakingly gathered, combed his hair straight, put on his feather headdress, and had Werowance paint an expression of stately welcome on his face. Then, with due dignity, he stepped forward to the pale strangers and spoke with appropriate gestures, accompanied by Ixtil's flute; then he danced in a circle around the fire.

"Welcome, you Spaniards," Temi cried, "for you are

men like us! You have come from a far place, no doubt. But now you are here. What we have is yours. We invite you to eat our food. Then you shall rest. And then, if you need our help for anything, you will tell us how to provide it. Be welcome to our village!"

A blunt and broad Spaniard stood up haltingly, without ceremony. "I am Lieutenant Pedro Fages, the leader of this company. I speak your language poorly, as you speak mine. That can be remedied later. But now my men and I are here to shoot bears. *Con vuestro permiso.* We hear you have many mighty grizzlies in this valley. It is so? *Si?*"

Chinichinic rose up. "Why do you come to hunt our bears? And what is 'to shoot'?"

Lt. Fages took a musket from one of his man and looked around for a target. A big black crow perched overhead on a branch.

"This is to shoot," he said, aiming and discharging the musket.

The explosion made Ixtil jump and it hurt his ears, as he dodged the falling bird.

"*Ai!*" he cried out, as did the others of his tribe.

"The reason why we come here to shoot," the Spanish leader said, "is that my people, at the place called Monterey, are hungry. The deer have all run away, and the seeds we put into the earth have not grown because of too much rain and too little sun.

"You cannot hunt grizzlies well with your arrows because they do not go deep enough under the hide. Then, being fast runners, they chase you and often claw you to death. We have muskets that pierce deeper and mules that run faster. Come and see our mules, but not too closely. Sometimes they kick or bite."

Ixtil and many others went to look at the mules, more of them than he could count, all tethered by ropes in a long line, eating piles of dry grass. Never had he seen such an animal, so large. He gazed at them and their riders with awe. Could the world hold such wonders?

A muleteer let him feel the roughness and strength of the rope. Also, he let Ixtil offer the animal a wisp of hay to eat.

"There is one more point," Lt. Fages was telling Temi and Chinichinic. "The noise of our shooting will drive all game far away, *pronto*. You will find none to hunt so long as we are here. So, in justice, we will divide with you the flesh we kill, provided that you give us a share of the fish your canoemen catch. Permit us to arrange joint hunting parties—your best hunters on foot to flush out bears or other game, we on muleback to run them down and shoot them. *Está bueno?*"

The two chiefs agreed that it was well. To get rid of the bears would be worth much trouble and risk.

Before they left the council fire that night, Ixtil and his folk first heard the visitors sing the "Alabado."

It sounded slow and sad, but was sung with a devotion which took away the sadness. Ixtil was to hear it often at evening in years to come, when the singers felt far from home and close only to their God.

Next morning, before the sun brightened the eastern ranges, the Spaniards arranged themselves into four teams of two men each, bestriding their giant mules. To each mounted pair Chinichinic assigned several of his best hunters to show them where the bears had been seen lately. Three of the parties went up the three smaller streams, before they flowed together, and the fourth party went down the big, full stream, after the junction, which glided westward to the sea. All through the day the sounds of shots from many directions told the women and children in the camp that bears or other game would be brought in before dark.

Naturally, Ixtil did not remain cooped up in camp with mere women and boys. Nearly a full-fledged hunter, he put himself among those who scouted the woods downstream. Like them, he put an arrow from his man's bow into the body of the big mother grizzly who was teaching her cubs to fish from a sandspit. Like them, too, he scrambled up a tree when she charged. The muskets of the Spaniards, coming up on their mules, had to fire many times before they killed her.

Their bullets, he noticed, penetrated deeper than arrows, but not much deeper. And many Spaniards did not seem to know where a bear's vital spots lay. They killed the cubs easily, of course, but a tough old male chased Muniyaut into the open and was prevented from clawing him only by their skillfully thrown ropes. Not so lucky was Cayatu. Thinking himself well hidden behind a large live oak, he was knocked down by an angry paw, and his neck broken, before a musket could be fired.

That ended the day's hunting for the downstream party. Leaving men behind to skin the three adult bears and the two cubs, they carried Cayatu's body back to camp, to the wailing women and the death chant, before burying it in the village cemetery, together with food for the dead man's journey to Hualtepec and his clam-shell necklace to pay his way there.

The three upstream parties had shot five bears between them. Ixtil's mind could scarcely grasp so great a slaughter of the deadly grizzlies in one day. He was shaken, too, by Cayatu's death. Before sundown, he and Werowance painted his likeness, purposely awry, on rock escarpments partway up the hill near the camp to deceive Sup. Ixtil liked hearing the Spaniards sing the "Alabado" again, before his family retired to bed in its permanent hut.

During the weeks that followed, grizzlies became scarce near the camp, and so did deer. Hunters had to walk or ride farther and farther into the eastern hills, until they were staying overnight and returning with their kills only the next day. Meanwhile, the people in camp labored long in cutting up the meat with keen knives the Spaniards lent them, reducing it to thin strips, and hanging them to dry over long trenches of live coals. That meant that firewood also had to be carried from increasing distances.

At the same time, the canoemen paddled their boats up the main river from the ocean with their catches of fish, which also needed immediate cleaning, drying, and smoking before they spoiled. Everybody had plenty to eat but none of the leisurely ways they were used to. Never before had the Chumash tribe worked so continuously.

Ixtil went everywhere and did everything. This was living! On some days he helped his mother and sister at camp. On others he went out fishing in one of the canoes, by invitation. But chiefly he was entranced by the Spaniards. He made a nuisance of himself—feeling their soft clothes and the leather jackets they wore over them when they went out to kill the grizzlies.

Greatly daring, he even fingered a musket, when he thought nobody was looking, and would have tried firing it, had it not been snatched away. The owner beat him hard, but this was so proper that he did not even cry out. He often repeated the Spaniards' words to himself, and grew to understand them and catch the rhythms of their speech. They tasted funny in his mouth.

He endeared himself to *Señor* Fages by carrying messages between him and the two chiefs, since he was learning more Spanish than anybody, even his older brother Tecocco, even more than his father Temi.

After that, *Señor* Fages would sometimes let Ixtil sit behind him on his mule's rump, hanging on with his arms around his belted waist. High up in the wooded hills, the *Señor* would sometimes tell him to jump down and would give him a message to carry, with utmost silence, to the widely scattered hunters. In this way Ixtil helped most in the hunting.

Finally, when Tixlini had yielded all its bears, the whole camp moved farther south to a place the Spaniards called Arroyo Grande, where another big river ran through many tall trees down to the ocean. Many grizzlies lived there. Before long, *Señor* Fages sent most of his mules back to his *pueblo*, Monterey, loaded with jerky to alleviate its hunger. He kept enough mules only for more hunting and for feeding the tribe of Chinichinic. So the hard work went on, as if it would never end, and Ixtil tired of it.

One day he was searching for pigments on the side of a rocky hill, close to the camp, when he heard noises in a thicket. He stole up to the thicket with his bow and arrow at the ready, hoping for a deer, but found instead his sister Erlinqua, lying with a Spanish soldier named Escobedo.

He was not ashamed for her. Couples who married in his tribe often did this ahead of time to try each other out. But Erlinqua screamed at him to go away, and when he asked how soon they would be married, Escobedo laughed harshly.

"Boy," he said, as if he did not know Ixtil's name, "not a word of this to anybody, you understand? Not to old Fages, not to your father and mother, not *anybody*. Or I'll beat you to death!"

Something was wrong here; so Ixtil asked Temi what ought to be done. That night, after supper, they both went to *Señor* Fages and told him what had happened.

"It will be all right if they marry," concluded Temi. The Spanish leader looked troubled. "That Escobedo!" he exclaimed in disgust. "He will never willingly marry your girl, and I have no power to force him to. If he married half the number of women he has seduced, he would be a bigamist a hundred times over."

"Then it is not all right, *Señor*. My daughter must not be made a wanton. Send the man back to your village called Monterey."

Fages nodded grimly. "He leaves with the next mule train, within three days. Meantime keep your girl at home, Chief. I hope what has happened will not sour the good relations between us."

"It will not. Even good leaders have bad followers."

That was how the affair between Escobedo and Erlinqua began. Would that it had ended there.

When no more grizzlies could easily be found, *Señor* Fages made packs of the last of the jerky and tied them firmly on the backs of his remaining mules.

"Thank you all," he told the assembled Chumash. "You have saved my people from starvation. God permit that we may help you equally on some occasion. That occasion may come soon. A holy priest, named Father Serra, hopes to establish a mission here to save your souls, and your bodies too. So I do not say good-bye, but *hasta la vista*."

Chinichinic answered for his people. "We are grateful that you have rid our country of bears, which did much harm. You will be welcome if you return."

The Spaniards' caravan of mules, laden with bear meat, plodded away in the dust.

The tribe resumed its usual occupations, but Ixtil kept wondering whether he had done right in betraying Erlinqua's misdeed to his father. On the one hand, as her brother he owned her a duty of silence; on the

other, he owed a duty of speaking, owed it to Temi
and to the customs of the tribe. Which was the right
way? Could a deed be both right and wrong? Why
did the Spaniards bring such problems of what to do?
He wished they had never come, mules or no mules,
guns or no guns. Finally, he settled down to hoping
they would never come again.

But they returned, after two full moons. Ixtil and
his friends were digging for clams on the beach during
a low-low tide when a runner arrived, panting out news
of the Spaniards' return to Tixlini. Following Ixtil's
example, the boys dug until their baskets were full
before dawdling back to the camp at a leisurely pace.

With a quick glance, Ixtil saw the same *Señor* Fages
and some of the same soldiers as before, including the
evil Escobedo. But two newcomers had been added,
both of them dressed in long brown robes with ropes
tied around their waists. They must be the holy shamans of the Spaniards who had come to save the
tribe's souls, and their bodies too, as *Señor* Fages had
predicted. One was a small, elderly man, not notable
except for his limp and his intense eyes. His companion was a younger shaman who seldom spoke but
walked always in the shadow of the other. They had
few mules with them, but the soldiers carried the
usual muskets.

The elder priest beckoned Ixtil, studied him with a
long stare of his stern eyes, and seemed to make up
his mind in an instant.

"We must have you as an interpreter, Ixtil," he
said briefly, "especially for Fr. Cavaller, who will begin the mission here."

Ixtil did not feel comfortable being seen through
like that and thought for a moment of refusing. But
one could not give an outright no to such a man.

So he said instead, "I think I have forgotten how to speak your language, *Señor* Shaman."

But *Señor* Fages laughed one of his hearty laughs. "What, after two months? Nonsense, Ixtil! Begin, and it will all come back to you. But pardon me, I'm forgetting the introductions. This," he said indicating the elder priest, "is Fr. Junipero Serra, *Presidente* of all the missions already founded or yet to be founded in Alta California. And this is Fr. Joseph Cavaller."

Ixtil acknowledged the introductions with reserve. This *Presidente* saw too many things of a kind not visible to ordinary people. Maybe even more than the spirits of the dead trying to get past Lord Sup. But Ixtil, at the same time, felt strongly drawn to Fr. Cavaller, who perhaps was a gentler mortal. However, Fr. Serra's voice was unexpectedly kind.

"We are looking for the right place for a mission," he told Ixtil. "It must have plenty of water, unfailing even in the dry season, fertile acres all around, trees suitable for building and for firewood not far away, the ocean near but not too near, and privacy—away from *presidios* and *pueblos*."

He smiled winningly. "I know I ask a great deal. It is my way. But at least I do not expect *el Dios bueno* to give it to me without labor. So you must show us all the surrounding country, Ixtil. I'll know the spot when I see it. One thing more: The mission must not encroach upon your father's *rancheria* at Tixlini."

For days, Ixtil led the two priests and their military escort through all the neighboring valleys, and up and down the hills wherever they enclosed large level grasslands that were watered by brooks. But always, after talking in a low voice to Fr. Cavaller, Fr. Serra would ordain: "Sorry, not this place, the stream will dry up." Or "The soil is shallow here. Not this place, either."

And finally: "Take us back to the valley of the three streams and two peaks, Ixtil. In the Lord's work we must be patient." So back they went.

Protected from the sea wind from the west, Tixlini lay on the eastern side of a green-clad peak. For the mission, Fr. Serra had fixed upon a spot on its southern side, in a grassy meadow graced with roses of Castile, as he called them, and many sorts of daisies.

Here he and Fr. Cavaller built an *enramada* of interlaced reeds, inside of which they erected an altar on which they put the sacred vessels needed for saying Mass. Here, as Fr. Serra inscribed on the first page of Mission San Luis Obispo's as yet empty book of baptisms, on September 1 of the year of Our Lord, 1772, the mission was founded. The two priests concelebrated Mass in the presence of Chinichinic's whole tribe, swelled by curious visitors from other tribes from Morro Bay on the north to Oso Flaco on the south.

First, Lt. Fages firmly set a flag in the earth with lions and castles on it. The wind made it flap continuously. Then the priests sang the Latin of the Mass loudly enough for all to hear, if not to understand. The soldiers gave the responses, also in Latin, and fired off their muskets in place of altar bells when the Host was consecrated. At the end, there was much blessing with incense and holy water, and more singing, including the "Alabado."

Never having witnessed a Mass before, Ixtil watched it all with fascination. The shooting drew his attention especially to the consecration and reception of the wafer, the Host. The singing pleased him too. In fact, his soul approved the whole mighty ritual. He resolved to learn more about its meaning from Fr. Serra whenever he got the chance.

The chance did not come, however. Right after Mass, the Spaniards became very busy sorting out

the cargoes carried by their mules into two piles:
one to be tied on the mules again, the other to be
left for the new mission. As Ixtil watched, Fr. Cavaller and the five soldiers under his direction carefully
rearranged their small heap into its component parts.

A hasty word with Lt. Fages confirmed Ixtil's guess
that Fr. Serra, accompanied by Lt. Fages, would
leave early next morning, with most of the soldiers, to
ride southwards to a big port called San Diego. Only
Fr. Cavaller, with his five soldiers and two so-called
Indios from Baja California (wherever that was), would
stay on to build the mission.

But the day was not to pass without further inci-
dent. When Temi learned that Escobedo was one of the
five soldiers assigned to remain with Fr. Cavaller, he
strode angrily to *Señor* Fages and Fr. Serra and nar-
rated what had happened between that lascivious soldier
and his daughter Erlinqua at Arroyo Grande. They
should not leave that man here to debauch his daughter
further, he told them angrily. But although *Señor*
Fages had promised before to remove Escobedo, he did
not seem to remember his promise.

Instead, setting his mouth stubbornly, he announced
in a loud voice: "I command *all* the soldiers in California, and I give them orders that seem best to me,
no matter what any priest says. Must I shift my men
here and there and everywhere because some missionary
does not like this man or that?"

Ixtil thought this attitude very strange. Looking from
Lt. Fages to Fr. Serra, he guessed that perhaps the
matter had become one of personal pride and power
between the two men, maybe also involving the two
priests against all the soldiers.

Fr. Serra's answer was mild but firm.

"Lieutenant," he asked, "what is more important,
your military jurisdiction or the virtue, indeed the

salvation, of this Indian girl?"

Lt. Fages did not yield. "Salvation is your business, *Padre,* I admit, but mine is to dispose my troops
so as to protect the province. Escobedo is not a good
man, I agree, but he is a good soldier. How many
saints do you think I have under my command? The
best I can do is order Corporal Briones to keep a
careful eye on Escobedo's intrigues with the native
women, and to discipline him accordingly. But Escobedo stays here."

Fr. Serra did not waver either. "This is an issue
which I must pursue with the Viceroy and his Council, *Señor.*"

Fages shrugged. "Pursue it, then. And so will I."

Fr. Serra turned to the impatient Temi. "I'm truly
sorry, but it will take some months before I can get
the right to remove Escobedo. Do not let your just
resentment light on Fr. Cavaller. Speak to him. He
can do much to protect your daughter. In return, he
will need your tribe's help to carry the mission through
the coming winter. Whatever food you can spare him
will be a treasure laid up for you in heaven by *el
Dios bueno.*"

Shaking his head, Temi walked away, unconvinced.

The party bound for San Diego, left before the
dawn.

When Ixtil came to the pile after breakfast, Fr.
Cavaller was already there, surveying the meager supply of goods. Through his worried frown, Fr. Cavaller managed a smile for the boy.

"Not much, is there, Ixtil?" he asked ruefully.

"Not enough for the winter, *Padre.*" Ixtil voiced
this conviction with sympathy.

"Perhaps just enough, with a bit of salutary fasting
now and then," the young priest suggested briskly.

"Let's see. Here's a fifty-pound sack of flour. Here, nearly a bushel of wheat for seed. Over there, a big lump of chocolate, enough for many a winter meal. And that box of brown sugar. Do you think your people would trade their edible seeds for my sugar, weight for weight?"

Ixtil felt very sorry for this priest with so little to eat, and without knowledge of how to get more. He said, "I enjoy sugar greatly, I think. I will trade you for seeds or other foods, but not weight for weight. I will give more. Seeds are easy to find, but not sugar."

Together they examined the three mules that had been left for the mission.

"I'm afraid they aren't very sturdy," the *Padre* observed at last.

"Not strong," the Chumash youth agreed. "Thin. Maybe sick. Not like the mules when we hunted bears. Maybe you should let them rest, each much grass, get fat. Even so, you could ride the best one to the ocean sometimes to catch fish to eat. I can show you the best places and the best bait."

The face of Fr. Cavaller had brightened somewhat.

"But what are those things lying in a heap over there?"

They went to look at the pile, so mixed that it was hard to tell where one thing ended and another began. The priest handled them carefully, as if they were precious.

"Equipment for agriculture and for building. Here, plowshares and points, hoes, and digging sticks, as used in Mexico. Here, machetes and sickles. And here, thank God, are three axes and a crowbar."

Ixtil hefted them all in turn.

"With these," the *Padre* said, "we can at least cut and move timber. No saws, adzes, hammers and nails,

though. No use trying to build much without them."
He sighed. "Ah, well, God wills it. The tools will
help in getting our edibles, not to mention our bodies,
under roofs before the rains begin. Maybe we can
even put up a crude church."

Ixtil examined the three axes with disbelief. He cut
his forefinger on the blade of one of them, it was so
sharp and hard. He stared in wonder at the blood.
Here was a kind of stone he had never even imagined
before.

"Steel," said Fr. Cavaller. "We use it in all our
instruments. Here, feel these hoes and machetes, but
gently. And lift this crowbar."

Ixtil felt and lifted them all again. How inadequate
his words to describe them! He could only exclaim:
"The world is so full of marvels!" Then an idea came
to him.

"*Padre*, if you let the men of my tribe use these
axes they will compete to cut any wood you like.
Steel! Hard, heavy. And what an edge it takes and
keeps! And how many different forms it can assume
for different uses! May I tell my people?"

"Of course. If you are right, we will begin by
building the church."

Chapter 3

When Ixtil spread the news about the substance called steel, all the men came, first to see it and then to use it. Tools made of it, unknown to their ancestors, turned their wielders into bigger and more skillful men. When the *Padre* announced that he wanted them to start by building a church, they clamored to use the axes.

To their surprise, he made known his plans—not for a sensible round hut with a hole at the roof's center but for an odd, square structure, whose walls were to consist of straight poles standing close, side by side, more like a council chamber. Well, they would give the owner of steel whatever he preferred. A grove of young willows downstream provided many straight poles which could be cut to the same length and set well into the earth, butt first.

Making a game of slashing with the machetes, Ixtil and his friends also brought armfuls of reeds from the marsh where the stream's water left its channel and stood still in a meadow. Weaving them tightly in and out around the poles was women's work, to be done by their sisters and mothers. Ixtil's mother, Maya, though expecting another baby in three moons or so, came with the other women. She was never one to let a pregnancy stop her. Besides, Ixtil had promised to make a new cradle board for the baby.

While the women wove the tules, Ixtil and his young men, acting under the *Padre's* directions, dug a broad hole near the river's edge, let in some water, and trampled the mixture of clay and water into mud, not too thick, not too watery. Everybody joined in plastering it evenly over the outer and inner surfaces of the walls. Strengthened by bits of straw and fibers from the reeds, the mud dried quickly into a thick *adobe* covering which the heaviest rains might somewhat weaken but not wash away altogether. More mud could always be applied to bare places as needed.

Finally, Fr. Cavaller asked for a straight, slanting roof , resting upon a ridgepole which ran the whole length of the building. The tribe had never seen or heard of such a roof, but after studying a sketch which he drew in the dust with a pointed stick, they managed to construct one. For the finishing touch, they thatched the whole roof with tules.

As soon as all this had been accomplished, Fr. Cavaller, now affectionately called Fr. Joseph, moved every article owned by the mission into one end of the new building: its painted tabernacle, Bible, crucifix, gleaming vessels, candles—down to the humblest worn tool and the crumbs of sugar in a wooden box. To the constantly replenished baskets of chia seeds and acorns, and the bearskin rug on which he slept, all gifts from the tribe, he gave pride of place just outside the sanctuary rail. Last of all, he affixed to the southern end of the rooftree a cross he had made of two gnarled pieces of live oak.

Then he sang a Mass of Thanksgiving. Most of the tribe managed to jam into the new building, which they had helped to erect, but some had to crowd around outside the door and the two windows, which were left open for the occasion. Of course, the soldiers came too. After Mass, Fr. Joseph gave the children the last remnants of the sugar and the chocolate. Then, naturally, there was a fiesta, with singing, dancing, and games well loved by the tribe. Fr. Joseph joined in wherever he knew how, and came in second in one of the footraces. Altogether a happy day, with much understanding and good will.

Completion of the building was none too early. A few days afterward, the first rains thudded heavily down. And soon after they ended came the mission's first clerical visitor. From the slight rise on which the church building stood, he appeared first as a tiny horseman leading a mule, far down the trail to the south. When he forded the stream in front of the mission, Fr. Joseph ran out to embrace him.

"*Hola!*" he shouted. "It is my good friend Fr. Dumetz. *Como se va, Francisco?*"

"*Bien, muy bien,* Joseph," said the friar, returning his embrace. "But the real question is how you are faring, without supplies or companion, in this solitude. I bring you a letter and gifts from Fr. Serra, loaded on this lazy mule of mine. The letter first."

Fr. Joseph read it hungrily. "But why has he gone to Mexico City?"

Fr. Francisco chuckled, his round face beaming. "Why but to ask the Viceroy Bucareli to decide once and for all who runs these missions, we or the soldiers?"

"I see." Fr. Joseph pondered, remembering Fr. Serra's dispute with Fages over Escobedo. "God grant that he may prevail."

"God grant it, indeed," said Fr. Francisco, "or military men will always be sticking their noses into our affairs, grievously hindering the salvation of souls. You must know, *amigo,* that in San Diego Fr. Serra, at the climax of a long dispute with *Señor* Fages, heard an inner voice telling him to sail to San Blas aboard the *San Antonio,* then weighing anchor for that port. He sailed on the impulse of the moment, leaving me as his deputy in these missions. So here I am. I am supposed to act in a ferocious manner and examine what you have accomplished.''

"After we have fed you, Francisco. Imagine our shame if you should leave here less rotund than when you arrived.

Fr. Junipero Serra's deputy laughed outright.

The two priests sat at a crude table outdoors, watched curiously by the whole of Ixtil's tribe. Having brought in the fish and the haunch of venison that morning, the people knew exactly what was being eaten but they wanted to see how, and also to hear these two holy men converse in Spanish, even though they understood very little of what was said.

Fr. Joseph told his friend that the gentiles had been feeding him and his whole party ever since Fr. Junipero had founded this mission, dedicated to the Spanish Franciscan San Luis, Bishop of Toulouse. "Without this aid, we must certainly have starved. Also, without them, we would still be cutting the poles for that building.''

"How many baptisms?" asked Fr. Serra's deputy.

"In the ten months, only one. A boy of eight years, and already dying when his parents presented him. If I could have saved his life, other conversions would have followed. But the poor lad was past my skill, or should I say past my ignorance, since I know no medicine but what is described in my compendium, *La Medicina para Los Pobres.*''

The priest looked gloomily at his hands. "At any rate, I saved his soul. He is the first to be buried in our *Campo Santo,* outside the east wall of our church.''

"The gentiles helped you build the church?''

"Not helped, Francisco; they built all of it themselves. I only gave the directions and lent a hand occasionally, when needed.''

Fr. Francisco put his arm around the bent shoulder.

"By winning their love and respect you have been converting them without dogma. They will welcome the teaching when you decide to start the catechism classes."

"I hope so," said Fr. Joseph with determination. "I'll begin with the boys, I think. They are most receptive to our holy faith. The older people will be hard to woo away from their tribal god, Sup."

Fr. Dumetz nodded.

After breakfast next morning, he rode away to the north, and solitude descended again on Fr. Joseph Cavaller. He took heart, however, after exploring the muleload of gifts Fr. Serra had sent: wine and tallow candles for the altar; for the reredos, a fine painting of the *Virgen del Pilar;* a sackful each of the seeds of beans, peas, and wheat; for projected buildings, several hammers and quantities of nails. Above all, a cock and several hens.

Fr. Cavaller thought of the buildings which would be needed as soon as the mission began to prosper. First, a waterproof hut capable of bedding two or more priests. Then a much larger *monjerio* for the teenage girls and unmarried women. Also a dormitory for the boys. A public kitchen. At least two rooms for storing harvests. *Caretas* for transporting them from the fields. A separate dwelling for the soldiers. Eventually, a hospital.

Most important, a large stone church. But for that he must have skilled stonemasons, carpenters, and workers from other building trades. Such workmen would not come soon. The line of needs stretched on and on, without end. With a sigh, he gave up such dreams and turned his thoughts to really urgent tasks.

Now that the rains had begun, he must take care that seeds for all the crops be put into the ground without delay. That meant plowing, planting, weeding, and possibly irrigating, if the rains should prove to be insufficient. The Chumash *Indios* had never practiced agriculture, nor had he, though he had sometimes stopped to watch farmers at work along the roads of Spain. From talks with Cpl. Briones, however, he had received the impression that the tough and scarred old soldier had not always been a soldier but had grown up on a family farm.

When summoned to confer with Fr. Joseph, Briones admitted that this had been his past. "My father booted some elementary lessons in farming into all seven of us boys. Naturally, I do not love the art, as he called it, but if you desire badly enough that I should direct the plowing and planting, I could do it for you, *Padre*. Also, several of my men will gain merit for themselves by exercising the art if I apply pressure in the right places. You understand?"

"I think I do, Corporal," said the priest, after some moments of hesitation, "but you must apply no kind of pressure at all to any part of the anatomy of any gentile *Indio* outside the faith. He and his friends will work, if they work at all, as a free gift to us. If you strike them, they will disappear into the woods at the first blow—and hate us Spaniards ever afterward. I think, too, they would take alarm if you drove your soldiers too roughly. Use only the castigation of the tongue, Corporal."

Briones smiled hugely. " 'Castigation of the tongue,' eh? An elegant phrase. Well, I know something about that kind of castigation, too, *Padre*. You will hear me at it tomorrow—if we start tomorrow?"

"Yes, unless it rains."

It did not rain. After the evening Mass, Fr. Joseph had passed the word to Ixtil, so that early in the morning not only Briones and his men but also Ixtil and his friends assembled at the broad stretch of meadow that had been designated for the growing of wheat. The Chumash lads had hitched one of the mules to the best plow in the storehouse, as the priest, after some experiments, had taught them on the previous evening.

Briones tested the soil.

"Friable," he announced. "Just right. Gather round me, my little ones. You see this heap of stones I have collected? They mark where the plow must start. I now put one stone down every ten paces so as to form a straight line."

He measured off a hundred paces, dropping ten stones, and returned. "If the plowman deviates from even one of the markers, he will have me to deal with! Following the plow will go those with hoes, to clear the furrow of grassy remnants and stones. After them walk the boys with digging sticks to make a series of holes in the furrow, about *so* deep and *so* far apart." The corporal held up his fingers to designate the depths and distances.

"Into each hole a boy drops one seed of wheat, and covers it over with soil, after planting. Use the blunt end of your digging sticks. Does your intelligence grasp so much, everybody?" He looked sharply around his small circle of listeners.

"Good. I see that it does. Now observe, indolent ones. About half a *vara* behind the first line of stones I set a second, thus. And behind the second a third and a fourth, until every seed of our supply lies comfortably in its own hole, well covered over and prepared to grow fruitfully. You are all ready? Forward, plowman! Make straight the way!"

Planting the wheat took them two days and part of a third. By that time, men and mules alike were exhausted, and Briones had shouted so many oaths and sarcasms that he could scarcely whisper. Providentially, a series of heavy thunderstorms then drove them indoors and allowed them to rest. For three blessed days the soil was too soaked for the planting of peas. Then it dried out under the autumn sun.

In somewhat less than a week, all the mission's seeds, appropriate to the season, were in the earth at last. Fr. Joseph offered a Mass of Thanksgiving to God and gratitude to the gentile *Indios* who kept Mission San Luis Obispo going. In his prayers, he promised that they would share in the reaping, as they had in the seeding.

After that, Ixtil had a little time to do some neglected tasks at home. Maya was too heavy with the baby in her to move around much. Borrowing an ax, Ixtil cut and stacked a pile of wood for her much taller than he was.

Nor did he forget his promise of a carrying board for the new baby. From a smooth, light slab of wood, washed up on the ocean beach, he shaped it, with his obsidian knife, for the child's head, shoulders, and body. At the bottom was a hollow, to be filled with moss, where the baby could sit and do its messes. He imagined it sitting there and gazing at the world it would have to live in, gradually discovering many tearful things and not so many laughters.

Deerskin thongs that he would fasten on the board would keep the new one close to Maya's body and teach it to feel safe there. Ixtil couldn't find a deer at once, but he brought in three rabbits, good for food and warm skins.

Erlinqua, he noticed, stayed close to her mother these days. That was good. He didn't expect to see Tecocco at home, for he was playing the grown-up man, had moved into one of the empty huts near the mission, and was deciding on a wife from among the maidens. Temi had gone off somehwere, not saying where. Ixtil had the unsettling fear that his family was breaking up.

The night arrived when Maya's baby started to come out, but not head first. It came out very slowly, with much pain and blood. Ixtil ran to tell Fr. Joseph, whom he thought of as his second father, now that Temi had gone away. The priest, awakened, quickly put some medicinal things and some holy things in a bag and ran with Ixtil to Maya's hut. After washing his hands, he tried to help the baby out, but somehow it was stuck inside. With murmured prayers, he kept on trying, while Maya screamed and screamed.

It seemed to go on for hours, but the priest could only bring out gushes of blood. Then he ran to bring in two women who lived in huts nearby. They couldn't get the baby out either, but only blood. Fr. Joseph knelt, praying, with tears on his cheeks. Then the baby was born, but without any breathing. Then Maya stopped breathing too. The priest, with holy water, ointments, and many more prayers, did not bring the dead ones back to life.

Having asked the women to prepare Maya's body and the baby's body for burial according to their custom, Fr. Joseph put his arm around Ixtil's shoulder.

"Come and stay with me for the rest of the night," he invited gently.

Ixtil went, relieved to escape the terrors of his mother's house. But the night gave him only bad dreams, not even the sleep of exhaustion. Several times he dreamed that a hideous Sup was throwing Maya's spirit back from heaven, and the baby's too. After one such nightmare, which brought him awake with violent trembling, Fr. Joseph took the boy in his arms until the trembling ceased.

"Let's go out and have a look at the stars. They often help," said the priest.

The two walked slowly together.

"Every star you see up there," Fr. Joseph said quietly, "is a sun like ours which rises behind the mountains every morning. Do you know who made them?"

"Hualtepec, the great Good One."

"We call him *Dios*. Can you say *Dios*?"

Ixtil repeated the name several times.

"But," he objected, "when people die and their spirits try to fly to *Dios*, Sup throws them back. He is doing that to my mother and the baby right now. This world is evil! *Evil!*"

Fr. Joseph paced along thoughtfully. "Ixtil," he said at last, "whoever told you that about Sup hasn't told you the latest news. *Jesu*, the son of *Dios*, has thrown Sup down into the eternal fires inside the earth; and since our *Jesu* is loving and generous, he shows all spirits who want to go to his Father the best way to go. He is showing it to your mother and her baby tonight, at this very moment. No, Ixtil, the world is never all evil, though it is often sad.

"In the morning, don't go out to your work in the fields as usual. Stay with me for an hour after your mother's burial. There is much to tell you about *Jesu* and *Maria* and the good *Dios* and all His saints. Shall we begin tomorrow?"

It occurred to Ixtil that Werowance would not like it if he listened to a story about a different set of gods, and he told the priest so.

"Werowance is my rival, then?" Fr. Joseph asked, smiling. "Would you be willing to listen to me even if he dislikes it?"

Ixtil sensed that he had reached a crossroads. He studied the priest's calm face. "Would you let me go on painting rock-paintings?"

"Certainly, if they are paintings about *Jesu*, or any

other holy person, but not about the evil Sup who frightens your tribe."

Ixtil nodded. "I'll shift masters and learn from you instead. I think your story must be truer."

Fr. Cavaller patted his shoulder gently. "Not truer, Ixtil, but simply true. We priests here at the mission believe our story is the only true one. You understand that?"

Ixtil nodded acquiescence.

Along the east side of the church, Fr. Joseph had laid out and blessed a *campo santo* for all who died at the mission. Many friends and relatives came to lament the burial of Maya and her baby. The two were put together in one grave, the mother holding the little one in her arms. Ixtil added her best water basket and all her finery, including her necklaces, her feather dresses, and her short coat of prime sea otter skins. Fr. Joseph prayed strongly as the dirt was thrown in.

All joined him in singing the "Alabado," which they were getting to know and love—halfway between hope and despair, it always sounded to Ixtil. He led the others in several of the farewell songs in the ancient Chumash, as was his duty. Tecocco, he noticed, stood on the outskirts of the crowd with a slatternly woman much too old for him, perhaps married, perhaps not. Erlinqua did not attend her mother's burial, and that was surely a bad sign.

Now that Maya's influence over her had been removed, Erlinqua took up again with Escobedo and became a known wanton, since he would neither marry her nor let her be. Much distressed, Fr. Joseph went to visit Cpl. Briones in the soldiers' living quarters, and too Ixtil along as the girl's only relative who still showed any concern for her.

The three of them sat on the portico. The soldiers

had built themselves a two-story *adobe,* with a jail on the second floor and living rooms and kitchen below. Ixtil took it all in with admiration.

"I don't want this man *forced* into marriage, Corporal," the priest was saying, "but your methods of persuasion are known to be highly effective. Could you exercise them on Escobedo? Not only are he and Erlinqua committing mortal sin in plain view of the whole village, but they are setting a bad example to others."

The veteran scratched his beard thoughtfully, but Ixtil caught a glimpse of amusement in his eyes.

"I have already used some of the milder forms of suggestion on Felipe Escobedo, but where marriage is concerned, his powers of resistance are at least equal to my powers of persuasion. If I slap him into jail, he only eats heartily, while one of the others has to do his work for him. What would you advise, *Padre?*"

Fr. Cavaller hesitated before suggesting, doubtfully: "If you happen to know the corporals at some of the other missions, perhaps you could arrange to exchange him for one of their men." He frowned. "Of course, we might get somebody worse than Escobedo, but I doubt it."

Briones guffawed loudly before saying slyly, "In truth, *Padre,* most of us in uniform, who have to live in these obscure regions year after year without seeing any women except the *Indio* kind, are greater or lesser Escobedos in our hearts, each in his own degree." The corporal grinned broadly. "Bring up enough willing females from Mexico and all your problems of this kind will vanish. I guarantee it!"

Fr. Joseph was not amused, and spoke with gravity. "It ill becomes you, Corporal, to jest about sins most offensive to Our Lord." His voice became sterner. "If you cannot control your men, I will have to do my best to guard the unmarried women and young girls."

"How, *Padre*?" Briones no longer seemed amused, either.

"By building them a *monjerio,* as at Monterey, a large house where all will sleep and work under the vigilance of a discreet older woman. You and your men will start the construction tomorrow morning at the place which I will show you."

"It is just," Briones agreed respectfully. "I will see to it that every soldier does his part. You will hear confessions before Mass?"

"Yes, but remember: those who confess will please God, not me. Remind the others of that, Corporal."

Briones knelt for his blessing, after which Fr. Cavaller walked slowly away, Ixtil following him.

Thereafter, every morning, while Ixtil learned his catechism from Fr. Joseph, he could see and hear the soldiers building the *monjerio* at the other end of the mission quadrangle, opposite the church.

In teaching the first elements of the faith the friar used a little Bible, bound in red leather. He would first read to Ixtil a short passage from the Bible in Spanish. Ixtil would listen well so that he could repeat it word for word in Spanish. Then Ixtil would say the same thing in the Chumash language. The priest would listen carefully so that *he* could repeat it in Chumash. Then he explained the meaning of the text and answered any questions that Ixtil asked about it.

By this method, Ixtil and the priest quickly learned each other's languages. Ixtil's understanding of the major doctrines of Catholicism came less easily, for there seemed to be no limit to their meanings. When you believed that you had reached the end of a mean-

ing, you could see another one, or more, waiting on
the other side. Ixtil often thought that if he had not
been taught about Sup first, he could have learned
about *Jesu* with less difficulty. But when he said this
to Fr. Joseph as they walked in the patio after a
catechism lesson, the priest told him he was wrong.

"You developed your sense of reverence, Ixtil, which
I find to be very strong. Now you must learn to
attach that sense to the right object, which is *Dios*,
Tell me once more: Who made the earth?"

"*Dios.*"

"Why?"

"Because He wanted to create something good, something to love."

"Does He, then, love everything in it? Poisonous
snakes, scorpions, storms that kill, diseases?"

"He has love enough for all those things."

"For people, too?"

"Surely."

"Even the bad ones?"

"He loves them, but not their sins."

"Does he love you, Ixtil?"

"Even me, but most when I freely do His will."

"You have a free choice, then?"

"Sometimes too free."

"Tell me about the misadventure of Adam and Eve.
. . . Now tell me what original sin is, and its effects. . . . Now the virtue of baptism. . . . Now confession. . . . Now the Mass. . . . Now the *Espiritu
Santo:* how can He be God too?"

Ixtil pondered that one. "He is called the Third
Person of the Trinity; but I do not understand what is
the Trinity."

"Do not trouble yourself about it too much. We
will discuss that when you are older, Ixtil. Now tell
me why *Jesu* had to become half man, half God."

Ixtil stuttered as he said, "You mean 'all man, all God,' don't you, Father?"

"Very good. I made a mistake. You spoke what is true. To proceed. How, then, could *Jesu* die? Why is his dying called a passion?"

Ixtil talked of *Jesu.*

"Is the world evil, then?" the priest asked.

"Imperfect but not evil, as I once thought."

"Ixtil, say whether our spirits need fear any god when we die."

"No; no god. Our spirits fly directly to the Trinity, without hindrance."

"But some do not reach Him?"

"Only if they themselves decide to turn away."

"Do you love God, Ixtil?"

"Father, I do not know whether I do, or not. Why did He kill Maya, and the baby, who hurt no one? This could be evil?"

"No, it is sad, but it is not evil. All living things grow old, or sick, and die. Evil is only when we purposely disobey God. God lets us do that if we want to, but He wishes very much that we would not. God permits evil but never causes it. And He permits misfortune too, but only to remind us of our dependence on Him."

"Father, give me some of your strong faith."

"I am trying to give it, Ixtil. Tomorrow, another lesson for us both. So, for today, ends our peripatetic catechism."

A month or so after the sun started returning from the south and Ixtil's fifteenth birthday had passed, another priest, whom he had never seen before, rode down from the north.

"*Hola,* Juncosa!" cried Fr. Joseph as he ran to embrace him. "So, finally, they let you go from Monterey!

Como se va, Domingo?''

Ixtil watched the thin, restless man in Franciscan habit throw himself off his mule.

"The stomach, it still does not behave itself, Joseph. It does not like the alien foods of this province. But when Dumetz offered to take my place in Monterey, the *presidio* could find no more excuses to detain me. So here I am at last! Tell me everything.''

"Impatient as ever, Domingo? Give me time to breathe, my friend. Come, let me show you the little mud palace where you and I will sleep. We have finished it just in time.'' The two priests walked off arm in arm, talking rapidly.

They arranged to take turns in saying the morning and evening Masses. Because of Fr. Juncosa's chronic indigestion, he took over supervision of the field work, where the fresh air and exercise would heal him. Just at this time, the *Indios* were busy hoeing the weeds among the sprouts of grain and peas. Fr. Juncosa saw to it that they hoed cleanly, without cutting the precious young shoots, and would often give a hand where needed. Also, he had brought with him lettuce seeds and nubbins of potatoes to be planted in their own places.

Fr. Joseph continued to supervise construction of all the buildings, first the *monjerio,* then the store-rooms where the harvests could be kept safe and dry, each in its own bin. These buildings were placed on the west side of the priests' house. Fr. Joseph also conducted the catechism classes, always expanding with new recruits. Likewise the care and repair of the church structure, the disciplining of *Indios* as needed, negotiations with Cpl. Briones about his soldiers, and all such matters close to home. In other words, thought Ixtil, on Fr. Joseph Cavaller rested the responsibilities for most of the troublesome work in the mission.

As it happened, the harvest of winter wheat was better than merely good: it was astounding. The 100-pound sack brought by Fr. Dumetz multiplied itself eightfold. The peas promised to do at least equally well. And the beans, likewise, planted in April by Fr. Juncosa when the frosts had ceased. So also the nubbins of potatoes and the lettuce, as the sun grew hot.

These agricultural triumphs allowed distribution of careful portions to each Chumash family that was living and working at the mission. Fr. Joseph made sure that all of them were present when the grain harvesting began and that all helped with the labor.

"See," he addressed them in their language, "how productive the agriculture is! Before, when you got your food only by hunting, you never knew whether you would find any beast to hunt, and often you went hungry. Here, you know what you plant, and when it is ripe you harvest the seeds. Some you eat, some you save and plant again. You can count the moons for each thing—for planting, for harvesting, and for planting again. This is the way civilized men live. God bless the harvest!"

Chapter 4

The presence of Fr. Juncosa in the fields allowed time for Fr. Joseph to visit each hut of Chief Chinichinic's tribe. He talked with the fathers and mothers and played with the children. To all he told the true story of *Jesu, Maria,* and *José* (his own patron saint) and how *Jesu* was near them every minute to help them if they prayed, and to take them to His heaven to live there happily after they died on earth.

But only if they were baptized. He explained carefully about baptism. Listening to him, most of the adults put on faces full of doubt about their own baptism but cheerfully agreed that it would be well to pour the water on the heads of the little ones. In this way, Fr. Joseph soon had twenty-five candidates for baptism from the home tribe, all children. He gave catechetical lessons to the older ones for an hour every morning, as he had been doing for Ixtil. He kept Ixtil for these classes, nominally as an interpreter of the languages but actually as an assistant teacher with whom the children felt more at home, and from whom they often learned more than they could from a grown-up who wore strangely shaped and perhaps formidable brown garments. When they had learned enough, they were baptized by the two priests at a Sunday Mass in church, in the presence of all the resident Chumash from Chinichinic's tribe.

This having been accomplished, Fr. Joseph asked Ixtil how many other tribes had villages within a radius of ten miles. When Ixtil found out what he meant by a "mile," he ticked off on his fingers this list of their names: Alijpa, Chatmnelt, Guajna, Nahuca, So, and Tipajpa.

Summing up, he explained: "Six small villages, six small tribes of the Chumash, from Morro down past Pismo. But some miles are longer than others, especially over hills."

"Good!" exclaimed the priest. "We will visit them all, you and I, in the name of *Jesu*. Fr. Juncosa has promised us two of his mules for the next two weeks."

That night, Fr. Joseph loaded the saddlebags of his mule with a handsome chasuble from Spain and all the supplies necessary to the saying of Mass, such as altar vessels, bread, wine, a small crucifix, candles, and a large Bible. To Ixtil's mule he entrusted a double handful of every type of agricultural seed the mission had. Also beads and small crucifixes for making rosaries. Lastly, of course, enough food for the two of them for ten days. Into Ixtil's hands he put a large cross, to be held upright as he rode ahead.

As they started off side by side next morning, Ixtil warned Fr. Joseph: "The people of every tribe we visit will expect from you a ceremonial oration. I know, because my father Temi, who for some reason has left the mission lately, was our tribe's ceremonial chief and told me about these speeches by visitors."

"Hm," said Fr. Joseph, reflecting. "How long should my speech be?"

"From one to two hours. My people are good listeners and expect to hear something worth listening to."

Fr. Joseph grinned engagingly. "This will be the first time I have ever had a congregation that will sit still so long. Depend on me to make good use of the time."

Toward sunset they enetered Alijpa, a well-ordered *rancheria* of about two dozen conical huts near the sea. Its inhabitants came crowding out to hear the visitor's oration.

Stopping his mule, the priest spoke in a loud voice. "I am Joseph, and I dwell in Tixlini, where, as you all must have heard, we teach about *Jesu,* the one true God. He helps you now in all your doings and will save your spirits after you die, if you call upon Him for help. I am His servant for life. I will tel. you the true story of this God *Jesu,* so that you may believe what is true, not what is false, as do those who tell you that Sup rules the world."

Fr. Joseph alighted slowly from his mule, took the cross from Ixtil, and stood facing them with it in his hand.

"The fact is that *Jesu* has driven Sup out of the sky to another place, and now rules the earth in his stead. Therefore the world is no longer evil but good. For this *Jesu* is not only strong, with all the strengths, but also good and merciful. He will listen to you whenever you pray to him reverently, and will do what if you ask good things. Listen well, for He sent me to tell you all about Himself, so that you may love Him as He loves you."

Narrating slowly in Chumash, the priest then began at the beginning with the divine making of the universe and of mankind by Yahweh, the Fall of Adam and Eve, and the consequences of their sin through all the generations of the tribes—indeed, of all men; the need for a Savior; the sending of *Jesu,* Yaweh's only Son; His coming in the shape of a man; His ministry, with stress upon His miracles of healing and the multiplication of food, as in the case of the loaves and fishes; His crucifixion and what it achieved for them, the people of Alijpa; His return to heaven but, nevertheless, His continuing presence in Alijpa to look after them.

"You see, then, that Yahweh the Father did not go off somewhere, like Hualtepec, after creating the Chumash. He is right here with you and me right now, doing us good. *Jesu* His Son, not Sup, was born on earth like the babies in the arms of the women who are hearing my voice. When *Jesu* grew up, like any man, He used His power to cast down Sup into the dark places, never to return. This good *Jesu* wants you to belong to Him. But to belong to Him you must first be baptized in water, as He was. Then you must learn how to live a Christian life. That is what we teach to all who come to stay at Tixlini. The two things are not the same but they lie close together: to be baptized and to live at Tixlini. I will baptize any of you who wish it. Then you can decide whether to go to Tixlini. May *Jesu, Maria,* and *José* help you do both!"

Nocsuni, war chief of that tribe, gave the visitors dinner as a sign of his favor. After the meal, Fr. Joseph invited the people to visit the mission. He gave to any who asked for one a rosary, with shining beads and crucifix.

Many asked, some to learn from it, some to boast of it or trade it away. Ixtil, for his part, having told the youngsters of his age that he lived at Tixlini, joined them in making a fire on the beach and sat there for several hours, answering questions as well as he could. Only after their return home did he and Fr. Joseph learn that twelve from Alijpa had come to the mission to hear more.

The priest's approach at the next four villages was about the same, and the success similar. Only at Tipajpa, the sixth and last village, near Pismo, did the two visitors meet a stubborn resistance. In the crowd that came out to greet them, Ixtil saw the faces of his father and Werowance.

When the reception of Fr. Joseph's address turned out to be less than warm, Ixtil knew why and, afterwards told him the reason. The chief did not invite them to eat with him. Over a small fire of their own they cooked the food they had brought with them. Only an eager girl of about Ixtil's age came to help make the fire and to offer food.

After they had eaten, Ixtil asked Fr. Joseph whether he would like to talk with Werowance, but the priest shook his head sadly.

"I hardly think it would do any good, Ixtil. Theological arguments seldom convince anybody. Werowance has a strong mind and will, I know. But he is using them in the service of a false god whom I could never accept and whom he will never abandon. Between him and me there can be no peace."

Ixtil nodded. On questions concerning the right God, he knew, the priest stood like steel. He didn't think that he himself could ever be so certain. There were still some old pieces of Sup and Hualtepec inside him somewhere, hard to get rid of as the new pieces of *Jesu* and Yahweh entered—even harder to fit all together in any reasonable pattern.

To his relief, the tall figure of his father strode out of the darkness at this point and stretched out beside the fire. Temi looked into it in silence, and so did Ixtil and Fr. Joseph.

Temi said at last: "I hear Maya died in giving birth."

"Yes. It was very bloody," Ixtil replied sadly.

"And the affair of Erlinqua with the lecherous Spaniard grows older, but no nearer marriage. True, Fr. Cavaller?"

"Only half true, Temi. We cannot force marriage, nor can we as yet transfer the man to another mission. But we have put your girl in the *monjerio,* where

Escobedo cannot enter. But these are not the true
reasons why you have abandoned your family."

Temi looked startled, then angry.

"No," he admitted forlornly. "I left my family and
my tribe because no place for a ceremonial chief
remains at the mission. Your ceremonies are not mine.
I came to the tribe of Tipajpa because here I am free
to practice my art." Temi's voice took on a solemn
tone. "Wherever the Spaniard will come he will trample
my art to death, and the other arts of the Chumash, too.
You will corrupt our lives and our ways in the end,
you Spaniards."

He got up and vanished into the darkness, as quietly
as he had come out of it.

"I cannot approve of your father's neglect of his
duties as a husband and father," said the priest sternly.
Then his voice softened. "But I can understand the
conflicts between his duties and his art. Perhaps if
I understood better what he calls his art I would be
more sympathetic."

"My father is truly a great artist," Ixtil ventured,
"both in the serious dance, which worships Sup, and
in the comic dance which derides him." He added
sadly: "He is right, I think, in saying that his is a
dying art."

"I hope, though, that he is wrong about us Spaniards," Fr. Joseph said. "We have come not to spoil
the Chumash culture but to bring the true word of
God, as Our Lord commands."

"Amen," said Ixtil, and crossed himself to drive
out the pieces of Sup still in his mind. Mostly they
faded, giving place to the brighter, more hopeful
pieces of *Jesu*.

Then and there, Ixtil knew for certain that Fr.
Joseph's substitution of a loving, merciful *Jesu* for the
cruel and evil Sup was the greatest gift that could

have been given to himself and his people. In spite of the loss of Temi's art, or that of any other Chumash. For to believe in *el Dios bueno* and in His *Jesu* is to realize that the world and its human life are good, whereas to believe in Sup made them evil, hateful, and poisoned with terror from beginning to end.

When Ixtil told these thoughts to Fr. Joseph, he agreed. "It is true, Ixtil, what you have said. To be a Christian is to see life as good and well worth living. But to worship Sup is to see it as terrible, and death even more so, since Sup still tries to enslave the dead spirit and keep it away from Hualtepec, its proper home, where it will find love and mercy."

"Perhaps," Ixtil speculated, "that is why our women bear so few babies, not wanting to bring them into a lawless world. And perhaps now they will have many babies in this good world you are showing us. And the tribe will not die out, as it is dying."

"You think far, Ixtil," the priest said. "I've often wondered why Chumash families are so small. We must tell them that *el Dios bueno* wishes them not to use their bodies in ways that prevent more births."

Fr. Joseph and Ixtil reflected in silence, watching the flames in the fire.

Presently the priest whispered, "That girl-woman who helped us with the fire and the food is back again. Over there, standing still in the shadow of that tree."

Ixtil also whispered. "Her name is Ysaga, Father. I inquired. If we stop talking, she may come."

They did, and she did, stealing closer till she was standing on the other side of the fire, darting glances of her dark eyes back and forth between them. Soon she sank down with a sigh of comfort, squatting on the earth.

"Who is your father, Ysaga?" asked Fr. Joseph gently.

"In the flesh? He is Chacuale, the maker of canoes in this *rancheria*. But it seems I have two others, not of the flesh. One is God the Father, about whom you taught us when you first entered our village. And the third is you, whom Ixtil addresses with much respect as Father Joseph. Therefore three fathers, not just Chacuale."

"How did you know my name, Ysaga?" Ixtil asked.

"Oh, I inquired." She smiled, her eyes alight with mischief. But suddenly she was grave. "Fr. Joseph, could you teach me about God the Father—here, now?"

To the lesson which followed, Ixtil added only a statement or a question now and then, to fill in the silences. But he watched Ysaga and her ways with his eyes, and with his mind he weighed her words and found her good. Moreover, she turned to him quite as often as to the priest who was instructing her.

Fr. Joseph brought the lesson to a close, remarking, "It grows late. Chacuale of the canoes will beat his daughter if she does not come home soon."

"He will beat me anyway, O my third father, who is God's priest." Ysaga laughed. "Before you leave tomorrow, will you baptize me and make me a member of your mission?"

"I will ask your parents in the morning. Normally we baptize a girl-woman only with her family's consent. About the rest, we shall see."

"It grows so dark that she may lose her way unless I walk with her," Ixtil observed, holding out his hand to pull her to her feet.

"May he, Father?" she begged, half teasing.

The priest blessed them both. "Walk with God, you two."

They went along the beach to the village, not touching each other.

"Do I please you, Ixtil?" she asked.

"You please me very much," he replied emphatically. "And I you?"

"You, and no other."

"When another year has made us both ready, I will come for you, Ysaga, if you are not yet at the mission."

"I will wait, Ixtil."

Arrived at her father's house, Ixtil took her two hands in his and kissed each palm tenderly. She did the same to his. They were now betrothed, by Chumash custom.

Arising before the sun, Fr. Joseph and Ixtil together sang " El Cantico del Alba," and the Father said his Mass. Then they ate a breakfast of *atole,* a mush of well-leached acorns, that Ixtil was wolfing down until Fr. Joseph reminded him that it would be unseemly to hurry their visit to Chacuale, the maker of canoes.

"Give Ysaga time to work on him," he added with a twinkle. "Even a woman's persuasions take time to work."

Accordingly, they broke camp and packed the mules before proceeding with due gravity through the *rancheria* to Chacuale's house at the edge of the beach. It was unusually large and finely built. Ysaga kept out of sight at first, hidden behind a screen of closely woven fern. But during the night she had so convinced her parents of her invincible determination to marry Ixtil that they raised no barriers to her baptism.

Ysaga, soberly receiving the blessed water, was a woman quite unlike the young minx who had teased the priest the evening before. Her parents and friends and relatives, who crowded the house to watch the ceremony, carried away memories which, almost against their will, would lead many of them to the same sacrament in due time.

Ixtil gave his future bride a rosary which he had made for his mother before her death. Ysaga asked him to put it around her neck, and he did.

As for her going to the mission to live, her parents forbade this for the time being. Surely the more proper time would be when the two young people were married. However, Chacuale would permit her to see the mission once or twice in advance, and Ixtil could come visiting her as often as he pleased, but only in the presence of her mother or her aunt.

All these arrangements having been settled, the priest and Ixtil started to ride back to Tixlini.

"*Por Dios!*" exclaimed Fr. Joseph. "The wooing here among you supposedly uncivilized Chumash is as stiff and formalized as in civilized Spain! I wonder that they let you visit the girl at all, before marrying her. Of course, only in the presence of *duennas,* those dragons of the *sala.* Still, the important thing is that you are winning an intelligent and devout wife, who knows how to laugh besides. Much better the strict rules than to leave the woman free to her passions, as in the case of your unhappy sister.

"I cannot help comparing Erlinqua and Ysaga. Night and day! Night and day! You forgive me, Ixtil, for talking about your sister in this way?"

"It is the truth," said Ixtil.

Chapter 5

As they rode up to the mission, Fr. Juncosa ran out, waving a square of paper with writing on it.

"A letter from Palóu, Joseph!" he cried. "It arrived yesterday by special courier. We have been impatient for your return!"

"Gently, Domingo, gently." Fr. Joseph smiled and alighted from his mule. "What does he write to cause so much commotion?"

"You phlegmatic one, have you no nerves?" smiled the other in return. "He brings with him Fr. Prestamero and Fr. Murguia to help you here. Also more *Indios* from Baja, some of them with their wives and children. Also cows, pigs, equipment—a long list. Now the mission will flourish. And you can send me home to Spain—to Spain, where I can sit down quietly sometimes and my stomach can be friendly with its food."

Fr. Cavaller surveyed him sympathetically. "Indeed, you have been getting thinner by the day. If we can persuade Palóu to release you, you may go. When will he arrive?"

"Having left Mission San Gabriel a week ago, he estimates two weeks more for the trip."

Fr. Joseph calcaluated rapidly. "So about October 16 he should be here, I think. What is the date today, Ixtil?"

Ixtil did not need to calculate. He would never forget yesterday, when he and Ysaga declared themselves for each other.

57

"The second day in the moon you call October, in the year belonging to Our Lord, 1773," he answered promptly.

"Well done!" came the praise. "We have much to do in these two weeks. Ixtil, ask Cpl. Briones and your Chief Chinichinic please to come to consult with me."

Then befell a great busyness. Parties went out to cut many willow poles and tules. Others got ready the *adobe*. The builders enlarged the priests' house; then they made a row of living quarters for the *Indios*, perfected with a big communal kitchen for them to cook in together. Then two workshops for skilled men and women who might disclose themselves. Next, more storehouses for harvests. Some pens for whatever animals might come, though their kind and number were not yet known. And around this quandrangle of structures the first wall of a stockade to enclose them all.

At this point in the labors, a watchman on the roof of the church called down excitedly that he could see a thick cloud of dust in the south. In due time he was able to distinguish three priests, riding in front of a long worm of people, and beasts winding behind them.

What greetings were shouted back and forth between Fr. Cavaller and Fr. Juncosa, standing on the steps of their church, and the newcomers, led by the businesslike Fr. Palóu! What *abrazos* when first they all stood together! What a concelebrated Mass of Thanksgiving for the safe arrival of the new settlers, attended by all of them, as well as by most of the tribe of Chinichinic, standing closely packed in the Church! Ixtil felt sorrow that Temi was not present to utter his oration of welcome. He would have been the leader of these great occasions.

That day, Fr. Joseph kept Ixtil constantly by his

side to run errands, since he (nearly sixteen and mature) knew both languages in use at Mission San Luis Obispo. He heard Fr. Joseph informed that Fr. Prestamero, like Fr. Juncosa, was in poor health and must go home to Spain, too. In their place, however, Fr. José Murguia would stay at Tixlini, a veteran missionary, a man of settled good humor and tireless strength of body. Ixtil, who had begun to learn how much priests could differ from one another, privately though that Tixlini would have the better of the bargain.

Going with a message to *Señor* Vicente, oldest of the *Indios* from Baja, Ixtil counted nine men, all Christians, to judge by their little crucifixes. Five were married and had brought with them their wives and children, who swarmed like grunion from the sea. The unmarried four had much eloquence in swearing at things that did not please them, and often laughed loudly at jokes Ixtil did not understand.

The married men, completely occupied in moving their families and goods into the living quarters just built for them, said very little. Their wives made most of the talking between themselves and their husbands, except when they shouted at the children, who also shouted at one another while they ran through the quadrangle playing games. All this provided a great sufficiency of noise.

An old question flashed into Ixtil's mind: Why were the *rancherias* of his people so much more quiet than this mission quadrangle? Obviously because of the smaller number of children. But that led to the deeper question, which he and Fr. Joseph had discussed round the campfire at Tipajpa, why the Chumash women bore so few children.

In contrast with the five married couples of the *Indios* from Baja, who seemed to fill the mission grounds with babies, a Chumash couple rarely had more than three—which sufficed to keep their population more or less steady, never increasing it. And in the years of great contagious sickness more people died than were born, Ixtil had heard.

He still believed that the ultimate cause of this infertility was the women's instinctive fear of Sup and his world. But did they, and perhaps the men too, eat in their food some element which prevented conception or induced abortion and stillbirths? If so, these elements must be unknown to his people, for he had never heard of such food being eaten on purpose. Anyway, Ixtil reflected somberly, unless the number of live births somehow grew much larger, soon there would be no Chumash left—only *Indios* from other regions, other tribes.

One of the youngsters from Baja threw him a ball in play and he threw it back happily enough. Soon he found himself in the middle of a game with them, his heavy thoughts forgotten. So long as children like these abounded, did it matter so much that they were not children of the Chumash?

Presently, Fr. Murguia, who had stopped to watch the game, invited Ixtil to come with him to see the mission's new livestock, some housed in stables inside the quadrangle, others in a large, roughly fenced corral outside.

Here was wonder! Ixtil had never in his life seen a cow, or anything like it. Yet suddenly, here in the corral, stood forty-one of these wonders, chewing their cud, and a few bulls and a calf or two. Fr. Murguia ordered Justin, the *Indio vaquero* who governed them, to open the gate of the corral and let the animals graze freely on the long rich grass outside. But only during the day. At night they must be locked into the corral, lest they stray away or be stolen by *Indios* from the hills.

The new horses should be guarded with even greater care. They consisted of four mares, one stallion, and four geldings, all of which should be kept inside the corral all day and fed and rubbed down by Justin's assistant, young Obregon. At night they must be brought into their stables inside the mission stockade.

Mules, Ixtil learned, came in two kinds, one for riding and one for carrying heavy packs. Of those for riding, the mission already had several, and now, for bearing packs, fourteen strong ones. The mules should be allowed to graze outside the corral by day, like the cows, and brought back inside the corral by night. There was not stable room enough inside the stockade for so many.

The five recently acquired pigs—another species strange to Ixtil—had their own fenced corner inside the corral, where they could wallow at pleasure. Ixtil burst into laughter when he first saw these funny beasts, with thick bodies and tiny upcurled tails. How full of fun *el Dios bueno* must be to create such ridiculous animals! Yet, according to people who knew, when rightly cooked they tasted above all others.

Fr. Palóu had not forgotten about the agriculture. In one of the storerooms Ixtil saw plowshares, shovels, hoes, rakes, and other tools for digging and planting unknown to him. And in the carpenter shop next door, neatly arranged along the walls, he found hammers and barrels of nails of many sizes, half a dozen new axes, several kinds of saws to pull and push, adzes, awls, and some mysterious pieces of equipment whose functions he could only guess at.

The great fact about them was that they were composed of the thing called steel which, as he knew from experience, could hold a keen edge for a long time and then be resharpened. How much still remained for him to learn! How clever the minds which could find iron and make it into steel, with qualities so superior to obsidian.

Ixtil was not alone in his admiration. As the news about these marvels of beast and tool went round the villages, not only the people of his own tribe but also those from neighboring tribes came day after day to the corral, the stables, and the shops to see and touch for themselves. They laid gentle hands on the heavy tools. The bolder spirits even went among the animals and caressed them cautiously.

Seeing so many visitors, Fr. Joseph asked Cpl. Briones to demonstrate the tools of agriculture, especially those marvelous ones which Fr. Palóu had brought. This the soldier, did with much skill and profanity.

Justin and Obregon showed the uses of their horses, mules, and cows. Through Ixtil's translations, they also explained about milk and pigs. *Con permiso,* they slaughtered and cooked a thin cow whose meat and bones were shared among the curious with all fairness.

The carpenter, Felipe, worked many long days in his shop making furniture, which required the use of every one of his tools. He freely gave tables, chairs, and beds to those young men who attended his work with most constancy and interest.

Now many of the men from distant villages wanted to stay at the mission in order that they might do the deeds they had seen demonstrated. The women, too, had much desire to remain. They liked the busy society where one could talk to women of other tribes and, in the communal kitchen, learn what they cooked and how. Also about their children—the ways of preparing for them, clothing them, feeding them, and—*por Dios!* —controlling them as they grew older.

Also, there was the *monjerio* and its perhaps improvable ways of guarding the girl-women while they waited for marriage to a good husband, if any such existed. Besides, they took comfort from the safety and regularity of life at the mission, and from sitting on the floor of the church every morning and evening, where they could look across the aisle to the men sitting on the other side, while the priest chanted and the incense smelled so sweet. Then too, a mother could go with her young ones to the catechism classes, which held their own pleasures. She learned comforting things there. Sup was driven away by the good *Jesu,* who would take her spirit through the golden gates of heaven, where the angels waited, and Hualtepec was always more merciful than just.

Soon every hut in Tixlini held at least one family, and newcomers were building extra huts. The two priests had many candidates for baptism. In early December, long before Christmas, they baptized forty, not all of them children. Had Fr. Murguia been more patient, the number might have been smaller. Fr. Joseph, Ixtil noticed, did not push quite so hard, and he loved the priest for it. In his heart he regarded Fr. Joseph as "his" priest, belonging to him, for whom he felt fondness and pride.

"Ysaga hasn't come, has she?" Fr. Joseph asked Ixtil one day.

"No. I looked for her in the crowds every day but couldn't see her. Her family kept her away, I suppose. This worries me—a little."

"Would you like to go see her this coming weekend? We can spare a mule for riding then, I think."

"Would I!" he exclaimed.

Before Ixtil left, the priest gave him one of the few sheath knives that Fr. Palóu had brought in his baggage. "They are useful not only for hunting," Fr. Joseph told him. "Women seem to find them handy for the kitchen, as well as for scraping and cleaning hides, I'm told." He blessed Ixtil. "Walk with God, you and Ysaga."

Ixtil knew what he would do with the gift. He would carve a small statue of the *Virgen del Pilar,* like the one that Fr. Joseph kept by his bed. During the long hours of riding down to Tipajpa, he thought of how he would carve it and how Ysaga would look when he gave it to her.

But when, at sunset, he arrived at the site where Tipajpa had been, it was gone—vanished. He looked around in bewilderment. To judge by the circles of ashes, every hut had been burned to the ground. In panic, he raced to the house of Chacuale, the builder of canoes. But it had been fired, too, leaving no sign that anybody had recently lived there. Gone also were Tipajpa's four canoes.

Ixtil sat among the cold ashes while, in the western sky, the glory died. Was it possible that the whole village could have crowded into those four canoes, with all its possessions? It was barely possible, because the canoes were so large. In what was left of the daylight, he looked for traces of a departure by land but found none. He would look again in the morning, but without much hope. Werowance and Temi had made an alliance, and had persuaded the people of Tipajpa to remove themselves from the "contagion" of the mission.

The sea was a great drinker of canoe tracks. He would never see Ysaga again.

Ixtil did not ride back to the mission next day at a gallop. Unspurred, his mule walked at a slow, meandering pace. His mind, too, wandered aimlessly from thought to thought, bewildered and bereaved.

Fr. Joseph received him wisely, with just enough sympathy but not too much. To keep hope alive he offered: "The next time a courier passes through, I'll send a letter to all our missions in California, asking whether they have any knowledge of the tribe of Tipaj-pa or of the names of Ysaga or Chacuale of the four canoes." He made this proposal with the voice of one desiring greatly to help, but Ixtil shook his head.

"Thank you, Father, but that *rancheria* deeply hates all missions. They will rebuild their village far off from any."

"Yes, I think so," the priest said sadly. "That is very bad, such hatred. I must pray for them. And for you, too, whom they have betrayed. However, you must not give up hope that *el Dios bueno* will reveal them to you in His own good time. In His divine fore-sight, He may even intend to make you the instrument of reconciling them to Him. Who knows?"

Fr. Joseph did not speak to Ixtil again about his sorrow. Instead, he gave the youth much business to turn his thoughts away from it.

At the Mass on Christmas Eve, Ixtil's flute from the tree of music led the people in their singing. With the help of Fr. Joseph, who knew all things, he had learned to play the hymns, such as "Alabado," which those in the crowded church knew by heart from hearing them at the daily Masses.

In the choir, in a clear tenor voice, he practiced singing more difficult songs recounting the birth of the baby *Jesu*. In order that Ixtil might play and sing so much music well, Fr. Joseph taught him at evening, after the day's work, the art of reading the notes that went up and down the lines on which they rested. So he came to love the sacred songs that soared so high. He was often called upon to play on Sundays and at evening services. But during the daylight he went back to laboring outside, as before.

That winter, the workers in the agriculture added more fields for the planting in order to feed the enlarging population inside and outside the stockade. They plowed more land for the winter wheat. They tried a new edible called corn, with seeds hard and reddish. They put three *fanegas* of this into the ground, with reverence. A small separate field was assigned to what had been saved from the bean harvest of the previous spring.

Best of all, the animals had multiplied, as *el Dios bueno* had commanded them in the Scripture. Instead of forty-one cows, the mission now had sixty-five, although a few had been killed and eaten at hungry times during the year. With sixty-five, they could afford to slaughter even more if hungry times came again. The five pigs, farrowing three litters, were now thirteen in number, although several piglets had gone into the stomachs of the people, with very hearty lip-smacking.

Not being able to reproduce themselves, the sixteen mules remained sixteen. But the stallion had been lusty in his maleness, begetting a colt in each of his four mares, for a total, with the four geldings, of thirteen horses. The geldings had been assigned, one each, to the four *vaqueros* who rode after the herd of cows, branding them and their calves with the mission's own design in red-hot iron.

Ixtil lent a hand wherever needed in most of these operations. In return he, like other lads of his age, was allowed to bestride a horse in the sight of the *vaqueros*. Soon he could ride well. For a time he planned to become a *vaquero*, when he grew old, like them. Too often, however, Fr. Joseph called to him for assistance, or for acquiring more knowledge of Spanish to improve his translations and more Latin for the Masses. He began to understand what happened when the bread turned into *Jesu* at Mass. In this way Ixtil learned how to serve, when needed, as an altar boy. For a time, he resolved to become a priest, but

Fr. Joseph advised him to wait a little, until he was sure he had a vocation.

In his dreams during sleep, Ixtil still saw Ysaga: he and she searching, each for the other, in vain, as is the way of dreams; but when awake, he no longer thought about her, except with an occasional stab of grief.

Then one day a courier rode up on a tired horse with the news that *Padre Presidente* Serra had returned from his trip to Mexico City and was inspecting his missions. He would probably reach Mission San Luis Obispo within two days!

A great stirring began among the priests. They hastened the instruction of six candidates so that they would be ready for baptism by Fr. Serra himself. Fr. Cavaller got the records and papers concerning the mission in the best of order for official inspection. The ailing priests, Fr. Prestamero and Fr. Juncosa, who had been unable to do any work to speak of, packed their small possessions in order to leave for Monterey with the *Padre Presidente.*

Briones drilled his soldiers. Since Fr. Serra would have a small guard with him from Mission San Gabriel, the corporal's professional pride had to be sustained.

Yet when Fr. Serra rode up to the church on his mule and descended to greet the mission's priests, who crowded around him, Ixtil found it hard to see how a man so ordinary at first glance, and with a bad limp besides, could have caused so much fuss. When all went into the church to hear Mass, however, and the *Presidente* preached a homily of magnificent sound and meaning, he began to see why.

During the priests' midday meal, which included meat raised at the mission, Ixtil served the food. Fr. Serra remembered him from the time twenty moons ago and addressed him by name.

"Ah, Ixtil," he said warmly, extending his hand, "you are growing into manhood. In holiness, too, let us hope. I did not forget your sister and that rascal Escobedo in Mexico. The viceroy has ruled that such a maker of trouble must be reassigned to another mission or to a *presidio* at the request of the priest whose mission he guards. We priests, not the military, are to guide life at the missions as a father guides his children. May *Dios* keep us humble in our victory!"

Ixtil stammered out his thanks and the other priests uttered an amen.

"What, though, of Governor Fages?" asked Fr. Joseph, breaking the silence that followed. "Will he consent to these changes?"

"It matters not whether he consents. He is being recalled to Mexico by the Viceroy for reassignment somewhere else," said the *Presidente*, so softly that he could scarcely be heard across the table. "This, too, is my doing. It did not seem wise to me that he should be kept here to bow to the missions, not he with his abundance of pride. But I begged Bucareli that his transfer should be without prejudice, with no blot on his record. The Viceroy agreed. Our next Governor will be Rivera y Moncado. He is on the way to Monterey by ship already. I would have preferred Sergeant Ortega, who traveled with us by land in '69 from Loreto to San Diego, but so rapid a promotion would have skipped him over too many deserving heads."

"Rivera, eh," mused Fr. Murguia. "A good soldier, but not excelling in tact. Well, we shall see."

After the meal, Fr. Joseph took Fr. Serra on a tour of the mission and of the Chumash settlement outside the stockade. From his many exclamations, Ixtil, accompanying them as interpreter, could see that the buildings impressed the *Presidente*. So did the number of Indians and their friendly demeanor.

"They look happy here, Joseph. How many baptisms?"

"In 1773, about 40, as I recall. So far this year, 23. We expect to reach close to 55 by December. So, for '73 and '74 together, about 95. The exact figures are in the book of baptisms which you left us on founding the mission. We are proud of our marriages too; not all Spaniards are Escobedos, and not all Indian girls are Erlinquas."

"Tell me about it, Joseph." The *Presidente* smiled.

"When Indian couples who are living together become converts, we urge them to be married in the Church. We have performed twenty-one such marriages. Also, three Indian girls have married soldiers of the guard. One has married a white jack-of-all-trades. We like this policy of intermarriages. All the races will have to live together in California peaceably from now on."

"Are all the inhabitants of the village converts?" the *Presidente* wanted to know.

"About a hundred of them are converts. We think that is about half of those who live here. The other half will either become converts gradually or decide to move away to villages that are still pagan. We hesitate to ask even one of them to leave. It would be harder to convert them later on."

"Very wise, my Joseph," the *Padre Presidente* said, "my steady and moderate Joseph. You have done wonders with the little I left you on the day of founding this mission. God knows I have often felt shame to remember how little. But it was a starving time, and I left you most of what we had. I entrusted you to God."

"He has never failed me since." Fr. Cavaller crossed himself reverently. "But you must not blame yourself. It has turned out well, especially since Fr. Palóu came with all those unexpected gifts." Fr. Joseph must have caught the twinkle in his *Presidente's* brown eyes, for he twinkled back, saying, "Don't think I haven't realized that it was you who sent the gifts!"

"I confess I did suggest to Fr. Palóu that he should pay you a visit with certain supplies, which I begged from the Viceroy Bucareli."

The two priests laughed together.

"Staffing our five missions is always a headache for me, especially when there is sickness among the priests and our House of San Fernando does not send replacements in time," remarked the *Padre Presidente* soberly. "I was never meant to be an administrator, Joseph."

"That I deny," said Fr. Joseph loyally. "But there is certainly much sickness among us now."

"*Gracias,*" said Fr. Serra, pressing the arm of his brother Franciscan. "I must tell you that Fr. Uson and Fr. Prestamero and Fr. Juncosa will go back with me to Monterey. All three are sick enough to require their return to our Mother House in Ciudad de Mexico. That you are reconciled to, no doubt, but what will hurt you is that you must also give up Fr. Murguia. He is badly needed at Mission San Carlos."

Fr. Joseph winced. "Indeed I shall miss him, Father."

"I know it. But this time you will not be left here alone to carry the whole load by yourself. God willing, Fr. Gregorio Amúrria will arrive early in July, for a year or so. Then Fr. Mugártegui, a veteran of the Sierra Gorda, will take his place. But best of all, Fr. Juan Figuér will be coming to you in August or September for several years, if I can manage it. He, too, served at missions in the Sierra Gorda—a very able priest, and humble besides. There are not many like him, and there will not be while priests are mere human beings." He sighed and said, "Well, enough about the juggling around of our scanty resources of priests. I wonder why so many of us become ill, in this mild California."

Fr. Joseph hesitated. He had only theories, which might not interest the worried man at his side, but he ventured: "In my little experience, Father, the chief physical causes are the foods, which are new to us, and the work, which is not only new but too much. The greater our success in converting the *Indios,* the more of them we have to teach. And what? Not only the truths and practices of the faith but also the methods of farming, of handling cattle and all the other animals, for by this knowledge they will have to earn their daily bread long after the missions are gone."

He paused. "But the worst cause of the sickness among priests is loneliness. Disturbing their minds, it disturbs also their bodies, which house their minds. Father, we are not *Indios.* This is not our homeland. We are thousands of leagues from home—Spain, Majorca. We feel it with every breath we draw."

"No!" Fr. Serra cried. "Where Christ is, there is our home! And among other Christians, new or old, we cannot be lonely."

"Ah, *Señor Presidente,* not all of us have your constancy and greatness of soul."

"If you only knew, Joseph! If you only knew!" Fr. Serra said sadly.

Ixtil, standing awkwardly by, heard it all.

After Fr. Serra left with his sick priests and with Escobedo, Ixtil began to pay more attention to the sicknesses among his people. Many lay ill of mysterious diseases in their huts. No sooner had Fr. Joseph erected a hospital, off by itself in a corner of the mission quadrangle, than these sick ones filled it.

For them, the priest now had a book in Spanish,

called *La Medicina Domestica,* which he studied by
candlelight in his room at night. He took it to the
infirmary with him on his daily visits, in order to
compare what it said with the symptoms he observed.
In that way he hoped to identify each disease and to
cure it with the treatment commanded by his book.
Always he took Ixtil with him, partly to help him
make the right comparisons but mostly for company,
Ixtil suspected.

The priest sometimes did not trust the book very
strongly, Ixtil noticed. Often Fr. Joseph would shake
his head and mutter into his beard. On occasion he
would hurl the book away angrily, with a malediction.
Then he would pick it up again and turn the pages
swiftly, despairingly. Sometimes he would read from
Scripture and pray. Sometimes Ixtil observed tears rolling down his cheeks. Then Ixtil would kneel close
beside him and pray too, for companionship.

It was true: the bitter medicines Fr. Joseph administered from the phials in his little box did not seem
to make much difference either way. Increasingly, his
patients refused the medicines, convinced that they would
kill anyone who ate them. The sick Chumash then
begged him to contruct a *temescal* with a fire to make
them sweat. But Fr. Joseph refused. He knew that when
they had acquired such a sweat they always ran, or
were carried, to one of the streams and plunged into
the cold water. This seemed to him an action of
madness.

So Ixtil took the priest into the meadows and woods
where the herbs grew, long known to his people. After
Fr. Joseph had learned the properties of each, he
tried giving them to a few of the sick. Being comfortable with the familiar herbal brews, their stomachs
prospered, and many were soon lying outside in the
sun, well wrapped against the wind.

Much encouraged, the priest administered the herbs to all the sick, with good success. Even so, two died, but that was the fault of the disease, Ixtil thought, not of the herbs. Such sufferers would have died anyway.

Soon after Escobedo left with Fr. Serra, Ixtil found Erlinqua in the hospital, her youth destroyed by some kind of evil disease. He crouched beside his sister's bed to comfort her if he could.

"How goes it, sister?" he asked gently.

She searched his face for the truth. "You can still call me sister, and mean it, after all I've done?"

"I mean it."

"Oh, Ixtil, do you think *el Dios bueno* is punishing me with this sickness?"

"Well, Fr. Joseph always says that *Dios,* being *bueno,* always has a large supply of mercy for those who ask Him for it. Shall I tell the Father that you would like to be baptised and make your confession to Him?"

Erlinqua slowly nodded her head. She lay for a long time with closed eyes. "I am thinking," she said, "that I caught this disease from Escobedo. He had it on his genitals, and said many others of the soldiers had it too. Now I have it even worse. Our people have never had such a disease before."

"That is true," Ixtil agreed. "I have heard, though, that over the whole continent of Europe, where the Spaniards live, the people have suffered from it for many, many years."

"They should not have come here, then."

"Perhaps not. But the evil they bring is intertwined with good. The Fathers have been teaching us many useful ways to feed ourselves from the earth and its creatures, and to understand the God who made them and us—many truths."

"I think I am going to die soon, brother."

"As God wills, sister. Death does not matter. What matters is how we die."

Erlinqua was soon another of those who died. With the help of a neighbor, Ixtil carried her body to the *campo santo* and dug her grave. Fr. Joseph intoned the burial services in the presence of many, especially of the sick who had recovered.

They left her under the protection of a cross which Ixtil made and set firmly in the earth at the head of her grave.

Chapter 6

Ixtil did not have time to prolong his grief. Only a few days later, a band of soldiers rode into the mission from the south, six or seven of them, on swift horses, not mules. These were no ordinary soldiers, Ixtil saw at once. At their head was a standard bearer with the flag of Spain, fluttering in the speed of his coming. Immediately behind him, on a blooded steed, galloped their leader. His eyes were fiercely penetrating, his face aquiline. In his helmet he wore a sweeping white plume and on the upper half of his body a cuirasse of bright steel that flashed in the sun. The men behind him wore the same half-armor, though not so rich.

Fr. Mugártegui took one look and shouted for all to hear: "*Hola!* The Captain Juan Bautista de Anza! Welcome, Captain! Welcome! Come down that I may embrace you."

The Captain sprang down and the two men gave each other the *abrazo.*

"You come like the whirlwind as usual, Excellency," laughed the priest. "Fr. Serra told us you were coming, but not so soon. Ixtil, call Fr. Joseph quickly. We have a most honored guest." Introductions followed.

"I must beg the favor of a night's lodging for me and my men, Fr. Joseph," said De Anza in a commanding tone which belied his words of begging. "Also, an early *comida* and a place to snatch a few hours sleep. We must be off again at dawn, on the

75

road to Monterey."

Fr. Joseph looked distressed. "I had hoped to keep you longer, Captain, and give you rest. Also to show you our mission, if you care to see it."

"Some other day, *Padre,* some other day," answered the Spanish leader carelessly. "At the Viceroy's request, I am finding out the best route from Mexico to California by land, and timing it besides."

"I see," said the priest, "but what ordinary mortal can match your time, Excellency?"

De Anza laughed heartily. "Why, anyone who can match my speed. But do not trouble yourself. Bucareli knows how fast I travel, and will make the necessary allowances."

The *comida* that evening opened new worlds to Ixtil. Serving the meal, he listened intently while the famous Captain told how he had led his horsemen around the head of the Vermilion Sea between Baja California and the mainland without wetting a single hoof. The route he had taken ran through the terriorities of the Yuma Indians, who consented through friendship mixed with fear.

Crossing the desert that led to Alta California, De Anza had emerged safely at Mission San Gabriel. "And here I am," he concluded with a triumphant smile.

"Having opened up a land route between here and Mexico!" exclaimed Fr. Mugártegui with admiration. "Now we shall not need the ships that bring our supplies, so slow and uncertain, so plagued with scurvy and sea sickness, as I know personally from sailing to San Diego on one of them."

The Spanish Captain lifted a warning finger. "Do not trust this land trail too much, *Padre* Mugártegui. The Yumas can shut it off any time they please. And even if they do not, a ship can carry more cargo than several long mule trains, and more cheaply. So I do not see us being able to do without ships on the California run."

So this man, Ixtil reflected, for all his dash and daring, seasons it with common sense. In him I see the *conquistador,* the type who, with a few hundred troops, overthrew whole armies in Mexico and Peru. Did he come to overthrow us too, who have no arms and no armies?

About half a moon later, De Anza stopped again at San Luis Obispo on his return trip southward, this time only for a meal. His mouth full of food, he said, "These Chumash between here and Mission San Gabriel are a remarkable people. I should like to talk to them. Can you supply me with an interpreter, Fr. Cavaller?"

"Ixtil is our best, and if he wishes to go you may have him, Excellency," said the priest. "But you must promise to send him back when you reach San Gabriel."

"I see you know me." The Captain smiled hungrily. "I might have taken him with me all the way to the Viceroy in Mexico City, who also needs interpreters. But I promise."

In order that Ixtil might keep up with De Anza's party, Fr. Joseph mounted him on the best of the mission's geldings. Riding just behind the Captain and feeling the power of his horse under him, Ixtil rejoiced that he had learned from the *vaqueros* how to manage a horse expertly.

As the party cantered southward along El Camino Real, hardly a royal highway yet but merely a winding path, thick with dust which flew up to fill the nostrils, a plan began to take form in Ixtil's mind. In one of the many Chumash villages ahead, he might find Ysaga. The more he thought about it, the more certain he felt that her tribe had moved south to be with its own people, clustered along the channel coast. There they would encounter the same language, the same customs, and even blood kindred, far from any missions to trouble them. Going north would have reduced the Tipajpans to a life among alien Salinan tribes, speaking a different tongue, living in different ways, and suspicious of strangers.

He would keep his eyes wide open for Chacuale's canoes, Ixtil resolved. He did not expect special difficulties in taking Ysaga with him, once he discovered her. After all, they were betrothed, and she loved him. Or did she, still?

That night they camped at the lake of El Oso Flaco. De Anza told his men, as they unsaddled, that this name had been given to the place by the soldiers of Captain Portolá, on their expedition to discover the Bay of Monterey, because here they had shot a disappointingly thin bear, which gave little meat.

"Also," their leader warned, "it is written that some called it 'The Vipers' because of its knots of snakes. Beware, *amigos!*" Several rattlers, in fact, had to be cut to pieces by the sword before dark fell.

"Where is it written about the snakes?" Ixtil ventured to ask De Anza.

In reply, the Captain took from his saddlebag a thin manuscript book. "Can you read Spanish?" he demanded. On Ixtil's nodded affirmative, the Captain handed him the book.

"This is a copy of the diary kept daily by Fr. Juan Crespi on Portolá's journey to Monterey, as is the way of priests who go with explorers into a new country. The Viceroy keeps copies of such diaries in order to guide the steps of the successors who come to open up the new land. He gave me this copy. Handle it with great care!"

Ixtil studied it well. Before he gave it back, he had memorized the details of the coastline ahead and the names given by Fr. Crespi to the Chumash villages along it.

"Gracias, Señor," he said. "I notice that Fr. Crespi has given a saint's name to almost every place where his Captain decided to stop at night. But often he records, as well, the names bestowed by the soldiers, who are not so holy. Which names prevail?"

"Well asked, boy!" De Anza roared, slapping Ixtil's back jocularly. "Sometimes one name, sometimes the other, it seems. Time tastes all the names and decides which flavor he likes best. He spits out the other. Nobody knows why. Now sleep. We ride far tomorrow."

They did indeed, in one day covering the distance covered by Portolá in four. They stopped for the night near a small village which Fr. Crespi had put under the protection of St. John the Baptist, because his feast day fell on the morrow. But the military men had named it Los Pedernales because of the rocky headland nearby, which provided them with excellent flints for their muskets.

Ixtil saw at a glance that the village possessed no canoes. He entered it, though, for a friendly chat.

The next day, De Anza called to Ixtil to ride by his side. "It is time I started to learn your language," he said soberly. "I have a good head for languages, but I do not love learning them. Strange, eh?" Here was a new De Anza, much easier to talk with than the *conquistador* version.

He asked Ixtil questions, and Ixtil answered each one, first in Spanish, then in Chumash. He made the Captain repeat the Chumash answer with special care for its pronunciation. Then Ixtil asked the questions in both languages, again with repetition of the answers in both tongues.

De Anza learned with ease. But his impatience, soon blazing up like fire, several times made him break off the lesson, until his will drove him back to it; and that in turn gave way to wrath, with himself, with Ixtil.

It was a stormy day for both the learner and the teacher. Consequently, the little band did not cover as much distance as usual.

Ixtil noted casually, in passing, a poor village known to Portolá's soldiers as Rancheria de la Espada because one of its dwellers had stolen a Spaniard's sword, which, however, was returned to its owner by the other villagers. Since Cape Concepción could be seen not far away as a low, bare point of land, Fr. Crespi had marked the meager stand of huts as Concepción de Maria Santissima on his map. No canoes there, either.

Next, to the south, was a larger cluster of well-made huts, called Santa Ana by Fr. Crespi, but by the soldiers Rancheria del Cojo because its chief had no use of his lame leg. Beyond that stood the even more populous settlement of San Seferino el Papa.

The number, size, and wealth of the villages increased as De Anza's party proceeded south. They camped that night in a broad valley, cut into by a salt-water estuary. Fr. Crespi had named the valley for San Luis Rey de Francia, but the soldiers called it La Gaviota, for they had killed an odd seagull there.

After supper, Ixtil found De Anza peering across the Channel at three shapes lying low in the water, their shoreward sides shadowed by the sun, sinking to the horizon behind them.

"Our first sight of the Channel Islands." He pointed. "Nearest us, San Bernardo. To its east, Santa Cruz. Then Santa Barbara. If I had a ship, I would like to sail out there and have a closer look. Some *Indios* live on them, I'm told. You see how they form a natural breakwater to keep the channel calm—and well protected, too, if artillery were mounted there at commanding sites.''

Not without ulterior motive, Ixtil reminded the commander: "There are plenty of canoes around to take you out there, if you wish.''

"Will they carry cannon?''

Ixtil had to admit in all honesty that he thought not.

"In that case,'' said De Anza, restlessly pacing the beach, "they can wait; and so can I.'' He smacked his hands together. "When I come back, that will be the time to borrow a few guns from one of the *presidios*. Slowly, De Anza, slowly.''

That evening's discourse often caused the Captain to pause to examine any canoes he saw drawn up on the sand, gauging their ability to transport various types of artillery. Such pauses gave Ixtil many opportunities to look for Chacuale's canoes. He felt sure he could distinguish them, since every maker of canoes designed them according to his own style, to satisfy artistic pride if for no other reason. He searched everywhere but could not find Chacuale's. He showed De Anza several cleverly hidden canoes that he would not have discovered otherwise.

After one such episode, the Captain eyed him quizzically for the remainder of the day. At the campfire, after dinner, he called Ixtil to sit beside him on the log they used for seats.

"Why all the interest in canoes, *hijo?* You cherish a motive known only to yourself, I think.''

Thinking quickly, Ixtil decided to confide in the Spanish Captain. When he told of the betrothal, of Ysaga's disappearance, and his belief that Chacuale's canoes would provide a clue to her whereabouts, De Anza did not laugh at him, or even smile.

"Ah, *amigo,*" he said with a sigh, "you remind me of myself when I was your age. I too loved a *doncella,* and she me. We would have run away and confronted all the world with our marriage. But somehow her parents learned of our plan and shut her up in a convent until a more suitable husband could be bought for her. Now she is the wife of a *rico*—very rich and fat, they say. But I came to the New World, where my eyes could not witness all that. They say puppy love soon vanishes, but I have not found it so. Perhaps that is why I ride so fast. I do not know. Anyway, if I can aid you, command me."

Ixtil was much moved by these confidences from so great a man. *"Señor,"* he said, "just let us go on examining every canoe we find. If they lead me to her, and she is still willing, I cannot imagine what trouble could ensue. If any does, I may ask the favor of your authoritative presence."

"You shall have it, *amigo,* on my honor. By noon on the day after tomorrow, we should arrive at a very big town of more than a thousand of your people— so big that some convoys passing there think it consists of two towns. Hence its name, Dos Pueblos. We will comb the place for you, not only its canoes but also its people. There, I think, we should at the very least pick up some news of your *doncella,* though not, perhaps, find the maid herself."

Comb it they did, but without any sign of Chacuale's canoes or of Ysaga and her family. Only when the ceremonial chief of the tribe of Siujto came in from hunting did they learn from him that most of the Tipajpans were on Santa Barbara Island, "Out there, Temi has taken your tribe to live, at Cajatsu, where they cannot see the Spanish convoys passing up and down on El Camino, here on the mainland."

"But Temi has no kinsmen or friends on that

island!" exclaimed Ixtil. "I am his son. I should know."

"Perhaps not old friends," came the answer. "But he has made a powerful new one in the person of Yanunali, our war chief. As is permitted by our laws to war chiefs only, Yanunali has one wife, with children, on the island and another wife here, also with children. When he grows tired of one, he crosses over to the other. Just now he is tired of the one here at Siujto. He will be back when he tires of the island wife."

"How soon will that be?" De Anza queried.

"Sooner or later," replied the ceremonial chief, smiling as he walked away.

De Anza watched him go. "I think I would go mad in your tribe," he told Ixtil. "Everything seems to happen by chance. Nobody plans, nobody organizes, nobody knows the value of time."

"Oh, we make plans when we must, and under orderly chiefs we attain order. But time is not our master, or our servant—as with you. It merely carries us along with it." Ixtil laughed ruefully. "But right now I wish I could shorten the interval until Ysaga returns to Siujto."

De Anza laughed too. "Perhaps it is just as well for your peace that we must press on southward early tomorrow morning."

"'Perhaps' is the word I must live by now," Ixtil said. "Anyway, I shall be back in camp by nightfall."

De Anza rode off with a wave of his hand. Ixtil turned back, walking slowly along the main path that ran through the village to see what he could see. He enjoyed being among the Chumash reed houses, far from any mission, far from the regulation of his hours, and far from the labor of learning and teaching. Of course, this is only a passing mood, he said to himself. Like Yanunali, I am weary of my mission wife and happy to rediscover my Chumash wife, though the mission wife, I love her best.

A hail—"Ixtil, wait for me!"—interrupted these thoughts. It came, he saw, from old Werowance, hobbling some distance behind.

Ixtil waited. He thought: Here comes the Chumash wife to fight with the mission wife.

"*Hola,* Werowance!" He put his arm around the old man's shoulders affectionately. "Do you come as a tempter?"

The shaman looked at him with disgust. "So you are even giving Spanish greetings now, Ixtil—and to me, who taught you before the Spaniards came." He shook his head sadly. "No, I do not come as a tempter against your new religion. Believe in that bleeding *Jesu* if you must. My faith is still in Sup, who makes others bloody, not himself.

"I come as one who warns. You have seen five of our people die and others lying sick in that mission hospital. The breaths of Spaniards are poisons to Chumash lungs; their bodies disease ours. They cannot heal by their prayers, for these prayers do not mount to Sup, the true. Nor by their unguents and herbs, which their fingers contaminate. Why this is so, only Sup knows. But the fact is that all who go to the mission die soon. If all go, all will die. There will be no more Chumash."

Ixtil remembered the death of Erlinqua, and especially what she had said about the disease of Escobedo and many other soldiers. Old Werowance had a point there. But Ixtil also recalled the hard labors of Fr. Joseph—his vain searches to identify and treat each disease as commanded by his book, *La Medicina Domestica;* his tears. Even back home, in his great nation of Spain, many sicknesses were incurable, Fr. Joseph had said. Ixtil must not let Werowance trap him by harping on a few deaths in many hundreds of perfectly healthy lives at the mission, nor by misrepresenting *Jesu.*

"Werowance," he said, "it is true that five of our people have died inside the hospital, but they would have died anyway, whether inside or outside. Many others have been cured, and almost all are so healthy that they have not even come near the place of healing. Likewise it is true, as you say, that our prayers do not rise to Sup, but the reason is that there is no Sup. Werowance, you and the shamans from long ago have taken away our gods and replaced them with demons. Hualtepec has not gone away but has remained to rule the world, justly and kindly.

"It is a good world, into which nobody should fear to be born. And when we die, His Son *Jesu* does not turn away our spirits but sends angels to carry us to His Father, So life at the mission is good, and death is even better because Hualtepec then takes us to Himself.

"You think too much of death, Werowance. Think more of life, both here and in heaven, with *el Dios bueno.*"

Werowance shrugged his thin shoulders helplessly. "They have taught you mimicry, I see; and like your father, you are a skillful fool. But you shall not have Ysaga to take with you to that mission of death."

"Depend upon my words, Werowance," Ixtil told him. "I shall certainly take Ysaga if she is still willing to come with me. And not to the gloom you imagine but, if God permits, to much happiness here and hereafter."

Separated by their creeds they parted, each sad, each silent.

Chapter 7

De Anza's party rode off again promptly at dawn, after a quick breakfast of cornbread and chocolate. By midmorning they had passed through the village which Fr. Crespi had christened Santa Margarita de Cortona but the soldiers Mescaltitlan, to remind them of Mexico. They stopped to breathe the horses on the far side of Laguna de la Concepción, where in former times Indians, sweeping down from the Sierras to the east, had wiped out two small Chumash villages and plundered them. This attack interested De Anza keenly. He spent nearly an hour learning from the war chief of the next village, La Carpinteria, all the details he could assemble about the number, weapons, and fighting methods of these *banditos* of the Sierras.

Meantime, as La Carpinteria had long been famous for the number and designs of canoes built by its artisans, as even the first Spanish explorers observed, Ixtil went to the beach to talk with the builders and to admire their boats, drawn up on the sand. They knew Chacuale, of course. "That man has a strong art" seemed to sum up their verdict of him. Yes, he had gone in his four canoes to the island Santa Barbara, but he had told nobody when he would return. Of Temi and his tribe they knew, and wished to know, nothing. A wandering people with no village of their own!

Ixtil watched how carefully the artisans grooved each board of their vessels, so as scarcely to need pitch to keep the water out. After thanking them, he ran back to De Anza's band, summoned by a shout.

That night they encamped near the village entrusted by Fr. Crespi to the care of Santa Clara del Monte Falco but known to the soldiers as El Bailarin, ever since Portolá's men had witnessed a chief dancing there. Ixtil had to explain to De Anza and his troop that every tribe had two chiefs, one for war, the other for ceremonies, which included oration and dancing. Portolá's men had seen the ceremonial chief. After dinner, a messenger invited the great white chief and his men to come to the village, which was a sizable one of some 800 souls.

"Do we take our swords, Ixtil?" inquired De Anza.

Ixtil was horrified. "No, no. They only want to greet and entertain us. We'll be safer without swords, or any other war gear, than with them."

While the Spaniards sat on long logs, the ceremonial chief delivered the customary harangue of welcome. With grave dignity, he told his audience of the greatness of his village, now and in the many moons of its past. The Spaniards, too, were a great people with a matchless history. Ixtil listened critically. This chief had more clarity and calmness than Temi but lacked his passionate eloquence. The serious dance which he offered to Sup was good in its way, too. In the comic dance which followed, this man did better than well, but he was not the born clown that Temi could be in this part.

De Anza chose for his gifts to the village's two chiefs three sharp hunting knives and a hand hatchet, all of which would prove enormously valuable to them and to their tribe. On the way back to camp he kept striking an ear with the palm of his hand.

"*Por Dios!*" he ejaculated angrily. "Those whistles have deafened me, I think. Must they always screech so loudly?''

Ixtil laughed, then sobered. "Captain, their screeching, as you call it, is accompaniment to the dance, which is purposely grotesque. Their dissonances bring to the ear what the dancer's comic posings, and his suddenly broken rhythms, bring to the eye. These are like the tricks which life plays on us.''

"You actually have a theory of art in these ceremonies?'' De Anza asked incredulously.

"Not a theory, exactly, Captain, merely a perception, struggling to become an art. So when next you witness a bullfight, or dance a fandango, or laugh at the jokes of a buffoon, perhaps you will remember the poor savage Chumash who also are striving toward art. By the way, I must confess that the whistles tonight were too many, and did not keep strict time.''

"My ears thank you for that admission, Ixtil. And my eyes apologize. They will watch more carefully next time.'' The Spaniard and the Indian laughed together.

From here on, El Camino Real began to swing inland, farther and farther from the ocean. Ixtil's last good chance to search the beaches for telltale canoes came at a large Indian *rancheria* in a fertile valley named by Fr. Crespi for the Assumption of the Blessed Virgin. But, as usual, the ranks of billows tumbled on an empty shore.

They traveled even faster now, for De Anza was anxious to reach Mission San Gabriel, where he would have to make his preparations for crossing the desert back into Mexico. Ixtil hardly paid attention to the surroundings through which they rode. Later, he was to remember only hazily valley after valley, which Fr. Crespi had carefully noted as ideal locations for missions. In this dry country the priest had named and

recorded every river or spring where water still ran:
the Springs of El Berrendo, where Portolá's soldiers
caught a wounded deer alive; the Spring of the Al-
ders of San Estevan, not far from the La Brea tar
pits, bubbling out pitch enough for all the Chumash
canoes in the channel.

Then, at long last, in the valley of San Miguel, not
far from the source of the river which bore the same
name, they saw, up ahead, Mission San Graviel. Never
having seen any mission other than his home mission,
San Luis Obispo, Ixtil was struck chiefly by the differences between the two. Here stood larger buildings, and
many more of them, though poles, *adobe,* and tules still
provided the materials. Also, this place seemed much
more crowded, not by priests but by Indians.

He could see several *rancherias,* scattered over the
valley, and could remember others in nearby valleys
he had just traversed. This whole valley was almost one
big *pueblo,* whereas Mission San Luis had only Tixlini next to it, and seemed more like a part of the
natural landscape in a region still uncrowded.

"It looks peaceful enough now," De Anza remarked
to nobody in particular.

"So," said Ixtil, not quite sure what else to say.

"Si, its founding, a year before yours at Tixlini,
gave trouble enough. We were told of it when we
stopped here after crossing the desert from Mexico. In
'71, Fr. Angel Somera and Fr. Benito Cambón arrived here to do the founding, with a pack train of
supplies and ten soldiers, an ample force. But the
affair was mismanged."

De Anza stroked his beard thoughtfully. "Learn now,
Ixtil, the follies born of panic. So many *Indios* assembled to watch the founding that the priests grew
afraid for their mission, and the soldiers for their
lives. It was decided that Fr. Somera should return to

San Diego with the empty pack train to ask Governor Fages for more soldiers. *Seguramente*—that took courage! But Fages, too, had his own fears, for Mission San Diego. So he said he could spare only two men. With these two, Fr. Somera returned hastily to San Gabriel. Having expected him to bring an army, the *Indios* had contempt for the few who came, as well as for the ten already inside the stockade, whose language they could not understand.

"On the pretext that a soldier had raped a Chumash woman—a charge that can never be disproved—they attacked the mission with clouds of arrows. So the soldiers charged out at them through the stockade gate. In the battle that developed, they killed a chief of the *Indios*. Then they chopped off his head—a mad action. We Spaniards do not cut off the heads of those we kill. Still less do we stick them up on poles to ripen, as did the soldiers of the garrison in their fury. Had I been in command . . . "

The Captain frowned. "I resume with reluctance, for the story does us little credit. Anyway, soon after the skirmish and the beheading, Governor Fages himself came to San Gabriel with a mule train and a strong guard of soldiers, on his way to establish a proposed new Mission San Buenaventura at Asumpta. You remember, we passed through that site a few days ago, under the name of La Asención de Nuestra Señora, bestowed upon it by Fr. Crespi."

Ixtil nodded. "I thought it a fine spot for a mission, *Señor*. San Buenaventura? A truly great Franciscan saint?"

"Next to St. Francis himself, perhaps the greatest, if one dares to guess the degrees of sainthood. Not a proper game for us to play, who are mere laymen in the Church."

"Why did this saint not get his mission?"

"Listen well. The Fathers and their soldiers at San Gabriel seem to have regaled the Governor with such exaggerated reports of their peril that they persuaded him to leave another half dozen of his guard for their protection. Too weak now to protect a new mission at Asumpta, or anywhere else, Fages abandoned that purpose and hurried with his remaining force all the way north to Monterey, in fear of an uprising by the *Indios* there against our capital. But *Indios* of that region, far from San Gabriel and speaking a different language entirely, had not even heard of the troubles here."

De Anza shook his head impatiently. "A tragedy of errors, Ixtil. The result? No mission for San Buenaventura. And a seething among the *Diegueños* here, which, in my opinion, will break out some other time at some other place between here and San Diego. But enough! We arrive."

The grimness of De Anza's mood vanished under the warm welcome given him and his party by Fr. Somera and Fr. Cambón. After a high Mass of Thanksgiving, all sat down to a table in the refectory, laden with several sorts of meats and—a particular treat—the first oranges and grapes to ripen in the mission's extensive orchards and vineyards. Ixtil had never tasted these fruits before. He took to them with relish.

After the meal, the two priests wanted to hear De Anza's account of where he had been, whom he had met, what he had done, and every other detail of his journey to Monterey and back to San Gabriel. Their guest answered all their questions with courtesy, often with charm, and did not question them too closely about affairs at the mission since his departure. Now and then he brought Ixtil into the conversation with a question or a reference to their common experience on the ride southward. Ixtil's Spanish proved fluent enough to cause him no embarrassment.

Not so, however, after the *comida,* in his efforts to talk in their language to the *Diegueños,* who were working at familiar tasks inside and outside the mission. So totally foreign to him seemed their tongue, and his to them, that except with the ones who knew some Spanish he was reduced to sign language, mixed with tentative stabs at words.

Hearing Ixtil's struggle, De Anza could not forbear laughing a little. "Forgive me, *amigo,* that I should be amused by the comic side of what is, actually, a situation for the greatest regret and pity. It puzzles me why the so numerous tribes of *Indios* in California all speak different languages, which separates them, as you have just been discovering for yourself. Do they derive, maybe, from some common root far back and now forgotten? And why are your Chumash tribes the only ones who build canoes? The *Diegueños* hereabouts go to sea on rafts tied together with fibers. They soon disintegrate, it is said."

Ixtil searched his memory. "We have legends of common ancestors who passed through on their way to Mexico, or possibly even farther south. Sometimes we even unearth their bones in ancient cemeteries. But where they came from, who they were—who knows? Perhaps they had the wisdom of canoes, too, but only we Chumash were lucky enough to have settled on a channel wearing a necklace of islands, where the water is calm enough for canoes." Ixtil shrugged and repeated, "Who really knows?"

De Anza spoke earnestly. "True enough, nobody knows. But look ahead, Ixtil. The tribes clearly need a common tongue. Shall it be a bastard brew of their many dialects? I say no. You *Indios* do not have centuries in which to learn how to talk together and with us Spaniards. Within a generation or two, we

shall be populating California heavily. Tell your people
to learn Spanish from the cradle. Then we shall all
have a unifying language. Possibly, also, a race unified
by intermarriage and by a holy Catholic religion, and
so by the same loyalties." He chuckled to himself, then
said aloud: "Slowly, De Anza, slowly. You look too
far into a future which may never happen."

The greatness of this man's vision won Ixtil. "I
hope it will happen, *Señor*," he said.

On first entering California, De Anza had left at
San Grabriel spare horses, saddles and other gear,
large containers for water, jerky, and other dried
foods, including fruits: in a word, all supplies necessary to crossing a desert and the territories of the
Yumas, whose intentions none could be sure of for
long. Therefore, guns too and ammunition in plenty.
When everything was ready for his departure, De Anza
and Ixtil embraced.

"*Adios, amigo,* or rather *hasta la vista.* Expect me
back in one year, or two years. The Viceroy will want
me to keep the overland trail open between Mexico and
California. I shall be very popular with him for a-
while, having done him a service. So I shall have room
enough to do a little bargaining." The Captain smiled
slyly. "I shall tell him I would like to take with me
many scores of civilian settlers who are married, with
children. Likewise, only soldiers who have families
with them and are pledged to make their homes in
this wonderful country."

Ixtil smiled too, but wryly. "Leave a little space for
us poor *Indios* who have lived here first.

The Spaniard reproached him. "You would not keep
it all to yourselves, the empty land? No, I see you do
not mean it. There is room for a hundred thousand
people—indeed, two or three hundred thousand. Spanish and *Indios* together. Can we not live together,

with justice?"

"With justice, yes."

"Find your Ysaga, Ixtil, to greet me when I come back."

With a cheer, the cavalcade galloped away, behind the King's banner, which flutter in the speed of the going.

Chapter 8

Ixtel's gelding, meanwhile, had rich grazing and much rest in the meadows around Mission San Gabriel. On the next morning, ready to depart, Ixtil warmly thanked Fr. Somera and Fr. Cambón and received their blessing and prayers for his safety on the road. This time, he resolved to proceed as slowly as need be to trace Ysaga, if she had returned with her family to the mainland. But what if she had not?

The idea of stealing a canoe and paddling it to Santa Barbara Island to rescue her entered his mind, only to be rejected with horror. Taking a canoe without its builder's knowledge was a disgrace not only to the thief but also to its maker, according to tribal custom. Into a canoe, the supreme work of his art, a builder poured so much of his skill and thought that if it was taken from him he became only a residual part of a man. He was, in effect, half murdered. And being only a half man, he could no longer occupy his highly honored rank in the tribe.

No, if Ysaga was still on the island, Ixtil knew he must wait until she came back. But meantime he had many places on the mainland to search for Chacuale's canoes and to ask among the shipwrights for news.

Knowing from his trip south that Asumpta was the first Chumash town he would encounter on the coast, Ixtil paid little attention to the lovely meadows through which he rode as fast as his horse would carry him. Before noon, he reached the *pueblo* named in honor of the Blessed Virgin's Assumption into heaven. There he walked his horse slowly along the beach, greeting the boatmen and asking for news of Chacuale. They could give him none.

At Bailarin, where the ceremonial chief had offended the sensibilities of De Anza and his compatriots, he again walked his gelding along the wet sands, amused by the memory, but with no better luck.

Ixtil had high hopes for success at La Carpinteria, largest and best of canoe shipyards, but because the builders were wholly intent on their work, they could spare only a few words to express their skepticism of his errand. Chacuale might have come, or he might not. Maybe he had landed to the south, maybe to the north, maybe not at all. They neither knew nor cared. Ixtil gave them up in disgust. He would ask among their women in the *pueblos* behind the beach, in the valley of the plentiful black soil.

Many of the women were busy washing in the clear stream which watered the fields, bright with brilliant golden poppies side by side with purple lupin. But a scrawny grandmother, who sat in the sun outside her hut, had time for Ixtil.

"I hear Chacuale has beached himself up that way," she said, waving her thin hand vaguely toward the north.

"At Mescaltitlan?" he asked.

She shrugged. "Maybe. Or maybe Dos Pueblos. The woman who gave me that morsel of gossip did not say. She is a very fat woman, *hijo,* and talks like a running river which cannot be stopped. She is. . . "

Ixtil interrupted as politely as he could. "It is enough, old one. I shall look where you say." He waved his hand, as vaguely as she had waved hers, northward.

She cackled. "No doubt you are looking for a fine, fat wench, comfortable in the bed, who loves her kitchen more than gossiping the day away, eh?''

"Exactly, mother." She was obviously preparing to discuss at length the qualifications needed in a desirable woman younger than herself. Ixtil fled.

Convinced that Dos Pueblos, where he had talked with Werowance, was the most likely place to look, Ixtil galloped through Mescaltitlan without pause and to the beach below the Two Towns. Ther they were!— the four canoes of Chacuale, in the rough cradles customary for boats under repair. He descended from his horse to inspect them.

"Ah, the beauties!" he exclaimed, surveying their art closely. Luckily, Chacuale was nowhere in sight. At the time of Ixtil's betrothal to Ysaga, her father had not been enthusiastic about her match with a young upstart who had no visible possessions and, except through his father Temi, no prospects of attaining an honorable place in the tribe at Alijpa. Well, thought Ixtil, little does he know the truths to be learned, and the plentiful food to be eaten, share and share alike, at the mission.

He walked about casually among the canoe makers like a friendly onlooker, admiring here, questioning there. Beside a builder who seemed disposed to be sociable, Ixtil squatted for a chat, in the course of which he adroitly inserted a question about the location of Chacuale's home. At such a place, he said, begging *el Dios bueno* to forgive the lie, he could best propose himself to the great artisan as a humble apprentice who wished to learn his trade. The lie produced the information he wanted.

Having Ysaga's whereabouts in his possession at long last, Ixtil went to scout it out unseen, and especially to fix in his mind the location of her sleeping bunk in the family hut. From behind a large sycamore he watched and waited, until he saw her stand in the entrance of the hut, then walk ostentatiously to one of the bunks against the hut's back wall. She knew he had come, and was helping him rescue her!

Returning to the gelding, which he had left with his friend on the beach, he ate a little food from its saddlebags. Then he dozed and idled away the afternoon hours, until the sun fell into the sea through a sunset of great splendor, closely pursued by darkness. When the night became black enough, Ixtil led his horse quietly to the tree from which he had watched Ysaga and tied him to it with a knot which he could undo swiftly. He stole to the back wall of the hut, where he calculated her bed should be, whispered her name, and waited.

No answering voice. *Por Dios,* this stealing of a wife required much waiting! Had he mistaken the place? Again he whispered, and this time he heard a rustling from the other side of the wall.

"I've been expecting you, Ixtil," she whispered. "I saw you peering so impatiently this afternoon."

"It is well," Ixtil said. "Ysaga, do you still love me as I love you?"

Through the opening he had made in the matted wall she reached for his hand and put it against her throat. "Do you feel it—the crucifix you gave me? I've prayed every night that you would come for me soon. I wish I could see your face."

"Then lean forward; you can at least touch it." She leaned into his unexpected kiss, and let her lips linger tenderly on his, then passionately.

"I have a horse, Ysaga. Get the things you want to take with you, but not too many for the horse. We will ride, you and I, to the mission, where Fr. Joseph will marry us. Do you trust me?"

"Would I go with you if I did not? I've been ready ever since I saw you this afternoon, my husband-to-be."

"You are wise, little loved one. Pass out your things, then crawl through yourself, and quickly. We must gallop from here until we are too far away for anybody to catch us."

She had reduced her necessities to one large bundle, which Ixtil pulled through the opening, then Ysaga herself. They stole quietly to the waiting horse. Ixtil tied on the bundle, mounted the saddle and lifted Ysaga behind him.

As he brought the steed to a gallop, Ixtil whooped with triumph as if to waken all the sleeping ones in the village. Ysaga added her shout to his. Until the gelding had carried them swiftly for a dozen miles northward on El Camino, the two remained tightly together. Ixtil could have ridden like that forever, feeling Ysaga's arms around his waist and her breasts against his back. But the horse was tiring. He dismounted, lifted Ysaga into the saddle, and trotted beside with one hand on the reins. Soon he slowed the pace to alternate periods of walking and trotting.

They went on like that until dawn quickened the sky and the earth. Pulling the horse off the road and into a canyon well hidden by mesquite, Ixtil smiled up at the woman who was his. "I could eat something. Could you, Ysaga?"

"Anything or nothing." She smiled back at him. "Whatever you say. All night I have felt that I have been riding along a black road with heaven at the end, and you near me. But you are hungry." She jumped down from the saddle. "Where is the food, *querido*?"

She rummaged in the saddlebags and prepared a meal. "Our first food together, my husband-to-be." she said shyly. "For that reason it is sacred to me. But wait until I cook meat for you. And *frijoles*—is that the right word in Spanish?"

Ixtil nodded, then listened. "Many horses are coming, Ysaga of the lovely name. Stay very still while I see who rides them." He parted the mesquite and glanced southward down El Camino, then ran back to her.

"Quick, repack the food! A high *caballero* comes with the flag of Spain, followed by other horsemen in formation. They will protect us to the mission, safe from robbers on the way."

Ysaga looked at him with skepticism but no sign of fear. "Do you trust all *caballeros,* Ixtil?"

"Not all, perhaps, but almost all those I've met. Your safety justifies the risk."

They waited on the roadside as the column approached and, at a loud command, halted.

"What *Indios* are you that dare to ride a horse of Spain?" demanded the high *caballero.* "Horses belong only to missions and *presidios.* Where did you steal this one?"

Ixtil kept his temper. "*Señor,* I am no thief but an interpreter lent by the Mission San Luis Obispo to *el Señor Grande,* De Anza, to help him speak with my people on the way to Mission San Gabriel. This horse belongs to the stables of San Luis."

Frowning, the *caballero* considered them for a long time without gentleness. "It is safe for you to say so, *Indio. Señor* De Anza already crosses the desert. He cannot contradict you."

"No, but the *Padres* at San Luis can, if I lie. Take me there and ask them."

The *caballero* laughed jarringly. "I intend to, my interpreter. And now let me hear your story explaining why you ride El Camino with this woman. She strikes me as a common *puta.*"

"No *puta, Señor,* but my betrothed, who goes to the mission with me, where *Padre* Cavaller will marry us. I invite you to witness our wedding, if you have eyes to see, ears to hear, and a tongue to keep silent." Ixtil and Ysaga laughed at the *caballero* in return.

In the presence of his soldiers, the *caballero* could not carry his exchange of incivilities with the *Indios* further, much less order them flogged.

"Take your place at the rear of the column," he commanded sharply. "Cpl. Cabrillo," he shouted, "I put these *Indios* in your care. See that they do not escape!"

Ixtil mounted the gelding and swung Ysaga behind him.

"I'm sorry that you must listen to these insults, *cara,*" Ixtil apologized. "One of these days I shall cut that man's throat for you." He asked Cpl. Cabrillo who the *caballero* was.

"No one less than Captain Rivera y Moncado, the newly appointed Governor of California," the corporal replied. "He rides to Monterey."

"God keep California and all who live here," muttered Ixtil.

The corporal heard him and roared approvingly. "Amen to that, say I, and all good men!"

When they arrived at Mission San Luis Obispo two days later, Captain Rivera waxed loud in his apologies to the young couple after Fr. Cavaller indignantly verified Ixtil's story in every particular.

"I am close to hating that man, Father," Ixtil confessed later.

The priest shook his head. "He needs pity and friendship, not hatred, Ixtil. Have you never before met such a man? He is not cruel but weak and changeable, as he himself knows only too well. In a position of authority, which he now has, and which is the worst possible state to befall him, he feels he must display a strength which will hide his defects. He feigns this display too hard and often, until he becomes a bully and hurts others, only half unaware of what he is doing. If challenged, he reverts to the opposite extreme and sickens us with his humility.

"Hated, lonely, ineffectual, he pursues his course until his deeds pull him down. He has been able and courageous as a soldier, and will be again, if not ruined by having been Governor. Pray for him, Ixtil."

Ixtil shook his head. He could not forgive so easily.

"Try," urged the priest. "In your happiness with Ysaga you can afford to forgive."

Fr. Joseph paused for a moment. "Two Chumash marriages will be celebrated this coming Sunday. Shall I add yours as the third?"

"Please, Father, yes."

"In the meantime, Ysaga will sleep in the *monjerio* with the unmarried girls and widows. The other prospective bridegrooms are allowed time off from work between today and Sunday in order to build their huts. You have the same freedom, if you wish."

With reverence and thanks, Ixtil accepted the dispensation.

Chapter 9

Calling for Ysaga at the *monjerio,* Ixtil took her the length and breadth of the village and its environs to choose a site where he should build their home. Without trees, most of the streets were dusty, bare roadways for the wind. But on the outskirts, upstream, grew a large live oak whose branches allowed sun and shade, their patterns flickering on the water as the breeze blew through.

A single look won Ysaga. "Here!" she exclaimed. "Oh, Ixtil, we can be happy here! Near the cleanness and the sound of water, yet not far from either the other dwellings or the *Cristo* on the altar."

Ixtil liked it too, because from where he was standing he could see the top of Mt. San Luis Obispo, rising loftily into the sky. Thence will come strength, he thought. Aloud he said, "Very well. Here I shall build."

Ysaga laughed and linked her arm with his. "Do not think, my sober one, that you will build alone. I too know the Chumash way, and have often helped my fathers and brothers. We have a ditty in my tribe:

> What's built alone
> Is soon gone;
> Built together
> Outlives all weather.

Ixtil hid a smile. "We too have a ditty, *cara,* sung to the same tune:

What's built fast
Will not last;
Not so
What's built slow.

So began four happy days, industrious yet full of
laughter and song. With ax, hatchet, and shovel, borrowed from the mission's carpenter shop, and with
Ixtil's keen sheath knife, they cut sturdy willow poles
for the uprights, bendable near the tops, the lighter
saplings connecting them together, the fibers of tules
for the tying, and the tules kept whole for the weaving
in and out between the poles and saplings. Finally,
the 'dobe for a plaster inside and outside to keep the
wind out and the warmth in. That concluded the cir-
cular wall of the dwelling.

Within, they built a bed frame along one side, raising
it about two feet off the floor, as Fr. Joseph did. The
bed consisted of strips of cowhide given to Ixtil by a
vaquero from a butchered cow. On top of the strips,
a mattress of many tules was laced together. For the
blanket, when needed, Ysaga provided a robe of soft
furs of sea otters, brought from her bed at home.

On the appointed Sunday they were married, with
the other couples, in a happy Mass sung by Fr. Cavaller, their priest.

During the next year, the one belonging to Our
Lord, 1775, the mission enlarged itself still more. It
was able to do this partly because the harvests of wheat
and other grains excelled those of previous years many
times over. The cattle, pigs, horses, and burros also
performed their duty of increasing and multiplying. To
so prosperous a rancheria, where the food became more
plentiful than the work, many of the Chumash flocked
from great distances. Fr. Cavaller and Fr. Mugártegui
baptized 146 people in that year, chiefly infants but

also many adults who needed instruction. Ixtil and his wife attended most of these baptisms, either as sponsors or as spectators.

But Fr. Joseph was troubled about something. One November day, after performing another baptism, he said to Ixtil: "I hope all these new arrivals are not coming just for the prosperity. How many are coming for God? You speak with these people, Ixtil. What do you think?"

What did he think? Ixtil was not quite sure. The families that came to dwell at the mission had mixed things in their heads, but it seemed to him that the things became unmixed after the people had been at the mission for a time.

"Many come only for the ease, or because their friends or relatives are here," he told the priest. "But without your teaching them about God and saying the Mass, they would get tired and drift back to their villages, or to the woods, after a little time. Whatever they come for, they stay for God."

"I pray that you are right," the pastor said earnestly. "Otherwise we in the mission might just as well be running an inn where the food need not be worked for."

As Ixtil knew and Fr. Joseph suspected, Ysaga's devotion to Jesus, Mary, and Joseph had been deepening since their marriage.

"Ixtil is right, Father," she assured him. "We of the cookpots thank the mission for the food in them, *seguramente,* but we bless you and *el Cristo bueno* for teaching us the way to heaven."

She hesitated. "I, too, shall be one to increase the baptisms, Father. I shall bring you a baby early in April, I think."

Ixtil looked at her in amazement. Her lips were twitching into a mischievous smile. "Little clown," he exclaimed, "why did you not tell me?"

"Big clown, so that your head does not grow too swelled up, like my belly. I think it better to tell the priest first. You will spank me now?"

"I would, were it not for the baby."

"The baby is not in that part of my body, husband as you should know."

Ixtil turned to Fr. Joseph. "You priests," he said gravely, "are lucky to marry never. Wives that make jokes! Living with them is like perpetually making the Stations of the Cross."

"They keep life merry, at least." The priest smiled.

"*Ai,* if only their jokes were better," sighed Ixtil.

That night, toward dawn, Ixtil was awakened by cries and running feet and by a red glow filling his hut. Jumping from bed, he lifted the large mat which hung over the entrance and saw flames spouting through the tule roof of the *padres'* dwelling. Even as he looked, they burst also from the carpenter shop, which housed all the tools for the agriculture, and, worst of all, from the rear section of the church. Priests, soldiers, and *Indios* were rushing about, beating at the fires.

Ixtil shook Ysaga awake. "There is fire in the mission, but not in the huts of the tribes. You and the baby will be safe here. Do not wander about."

She saw the severity in his face. "I will stay here," she promised.

Ixtil ran first to the priests' quarters, which were being wholly eaten up. Could any of the priests be trapped inside? He heard Fr. Joseph issuing quick commands at the church, Fr . Mugártegui near the shops, and the newly arrived Fr. Juan Figuér at the *monjerio.*

He ran to the church. Fr. Joseph, he found, had

organized a line of men stretching to the river to pass jars brimming with water, which two men on the roof dashed on the flames. The priest was wielding an ax to cut away the burning parts and the unburned parts which already smoked with the heat.

Ixtil spelled Fr. Cavaller at heaving the ax until, because of the water and the ax, the flames extinguished themselves. The carpenter shop, with all its valuable tools, had already burned to the ground when he ran there next, but, with the ax, he joined the defense of the granaries until they were safe.

Daylight showed a scene of devastation. Every mission structure except the church and the granaries lay in ashes.

"All that work," grieved Fr. Joseph, "gone in a few hours." He lifted his face toward the sky. "God in heaven, Thy will be done on earth also. Help me to be patient." He passed his hand across his tired face.

"Let me think what must be done first. Yes, the wine, the hosts, the candles, all were kept in that chest of drawers in my room. All consumed. No Masses can be said today."

Fr. Cavaller consulted with Fr. Mugártegui and Fr. Figuér, and Ixtil could see a general nodding of heads. Then Fr. Joseph told Ixtil: "You must ride immediately to Mission San Antonio to borrow the necessities for saying Mass. I will give you a note to Fr. Sitjar and Fr. Pieras, telling what has happened. Get from the *vaqueros* the fastest horse we own. Have you had breakfast? No, of course not. Nobody has had time for food."

"Do not trouble yourself Father," Ixtil said reassuringly. "Ysaga is efficient and wise. She will see that I have not only breakfast but enough jerky and dried fruit to last me the entire trip. But before I leave, I must warn that I think the fires were not accidental."

"Not accidental?"

"During the fighting of the fires I could see, as could others, burning arrows descending upon the roofs. And I use the word 'warn' because Werowance, the shaman of my tribe of Chinichinic, has been offended and vengeful since I, who used to be his pupil, have abandoned him and his god, Sup, to come to you and the good *Jesu*. I suspect that he led the fire raid. The others could have been some of my tribe who have not yet come to live at the mission. Or possibly from tribes over the mountains who have been enemies of the Chumash for long generations."

"*Gracias,* Ixtil. We'll take precautions. Now go with God."

Within half an hour Ixtil was riding up the newly discovered Cuesta Pass into the valley of the Salinas River. He had heard that the road northward along this valley had much dust and heat; but that was in summer and early autumn. Now, since the rains had begun, the greening grass refreshed his eyes and the wind of his riding cooled his face. He had never been in this country before, even in tribal days before the Spaniards came. It belonged to the Salinan tribes, who spoke a language without worth, which no Chumash would demean himself to learn. Also, the Salinans did not know how to build canoes, and were altogether a savage lot.

He rode with watchful eyes, and kept the stallion fresh by causing it to trot, occasionally even to walk, between gallops.

For two hours at dusk, Ixtil stopped to eat, less for himself than for his animal, which also needed to drink from the river and to browse in the succulent grass, unwearied by a saddle.

A good rubdown, then resaddling, and they were

off again. Luckily, a half-moon showed the path clearly; so Ixtil was able to maintain a steady canter, varied by gallops and intervals of walking, during the night. Where El Camino turned westward for the Mission San Antonio, the way became hard to distinguish. But by midmorning he was galloping into the mission grounds, straight to the dwelling of the priests, as described to him.

To Fr. Sitjar, who was teaching a group of boys in a strange tongue, Ixtil delivered Fr. Joseph's letter. The priest immediately dismissed his class and took Ixtil into the church to collect a package of the materials needed in saying the Mass. That done, Fr. Sitjar turned his attention to Ixtil.

"You will stay for lunch with us, of course."

"No, Father. I must hurry back. We need the Mass at San Luis Obispo."

Fr. Sitjar looked almost like a prototype of the priests Fr. Joseph had been reading to Ixtil about in the holy legends: jolly, rotund, with a passion for eating which coated the true holiness underneath.

"But no, my son," he protested. "You must break bread with us. We have a proverb, 'Before journeys, always the *comida.*' You will not make us violate the laws of hospitality? Besides, the food will give you strength to ride so fast that your mission will have the twilight Mass tomorrow." Ixtil wanted to believe that it would be so.

At the *comida,* sitting at table with the two Franciscan friars, he told them about the fire and with how much hunger it had burned, in whole or part, most of the constructions at San Luis. Fr. Sitjar made compassionate noises through his mouthfuls, but Fr. Pieras, a thin, busy man, of practical affairs and perhaps not such tender feelings, preserved a silence until the end of the meal.

"Have you noticed the roofing of our church here?" Fr. Pieras asked suddenly.

Ixtil thought for a moment. "You mean the red stones on the top?"

"Yes. However, they are not stones but tiles. I will show you how to make them, so that you can explain the method to Fr. Joseph. He will have no more fires. Tiles do not burn."

Fr. Pieras took Ixtil to the place where tiles were being made by many *Indios*. Some stamped wetted *adobe* and other ingredients to the right consistency. Others then modeled this mixture around short, gently tapering lengths of wood. When properly dried in the sun, the molded tiles could be taken from the wood and baked in the heat of an oven. Then came the laying out of them in long rows under a beneficial sun.

Fr. Pieras put two of the finished products, smooth and heavy, into Ixtil's hands. "Of course," the priest said, "they must be laid on a sloping roof of boards fitted tightly together, and they must be fitted properly to one another, the big semicircle of each tile resting upon the smaller, tapering semicircle of the one below it. Thus the rain cannot enter, nor the fire, either."

"I see," Ixtil said. "It is a very great work. But do not your walls have to be very strong to support such a heaviness?" He hefted the two tiles. "These are not without weight, Father."

"Yes indeed; the walls must be made strong if tiles are to be used. Tell Fr. Joseph to install larger uprights. Also, he should remember that the roof must slope *gently*. Come, I'll write him a note giving the specifications."

"And there will be no more fires?"

"None from outside, so long as no part of the roof is left uncovered by tiles."

The note for Fr. Joseph was scribbled at the rectory

table and received by Ixtil gratefully. As he gave Ixtil
the folded paper, Fr. Pieras' thin lips curved in a smile.

"Do not give us too much credit for tiles. We did
not invent them, you know. They have been used by
other missionaries in many places for many years,
wherever the danger of fire is great, as it is with our
flimsy wooden structures."

"Nevertheless, this is a great wonder, deserving the
thanks of the heart."

"Vaya con Dios, Ixtil."

"And you with His mercy, Father."

Ixtil rode into the mission at Tixlini, as Fr. Sitjar
had foreseen, before the time of the twilight Mass.

Fr. Joseph greeted him with a glad cry. "Welcome!
Welcome! Like a belated Magus, you bring gifts which
will enable us to see Christ again at the altar, and to
worship Him, as he decreed at the Last Supper."

Through the church doors, blackened by fire, under
the roof with its large, gaping hole, surged such a
crowd of worshipers that they occupied every inch
of the floor, standing shoulder to shoulder for Mass.
The mission lay in ruins around them, but the people
were in a mood to rejoice. They had come out on the
other side of disaster and had not lost anything of true
importance.

"You see," said Ixtil to Fr. Joseph, as he gave him
the note from Fr. Pieras, "the people have not joined
the mission because of ease but because of God."

The priest nodded gratefully.

Ruefully, Ixtil admitted: "Father, I am very sore
from all that riding, and tired enough to fall asleep
while standing. But tomorrow, if you wish, I will
show the people about the tiles."

Ysaga took his arm as they walked to their house.
"I did not expect to marry a hero," she said with

gentle mischief.

"I am too tired for jesting, *carita*. Let it rest until I have rested."

"Tonight, husband, you shall rest even from me."

The next week was remembered at the Mission San Luis Obispo as the Week of the Tiles. To a huge circle of workers who surrounded him on the first morning, Ixtil explained and demonstrated, as well as he could, how to make the tiles step by step. He picked teams of men and women to conduct each step properly. Each team, when shown what materials it would require, collected them. After carpenters had enclosed large stamping pits in walls of wood, the stampers brought water to make the *adobe* viscous, and added tule straws to harden it and prevent its breaking. Then the stamping began.

Meanwhile, modelers sawed logs of the right girth and length, split them down the middle lengthwise, smoothed and tapered them so as to produce molds over which the treated *adobe* could be thickly smeared. After enough exposure to the hot sunlight, the clay was carefully lifted off and fired to a perfect hardness in kilns built for the purpose. The resulting tiles were then laid out in long rows ready for use.

Reconstruction of the church building occupied the mission's three priests. They sent parties of men with axes into the woods to cut down and bring back tree trunks of substantial size and hardness to serve as uprights in strengthening the walls. Other gangs sought and found timbers of varying weight, some suitable for a gently sloping roof, some for rafters, and some for the lengthwise boards on which the tiles would rest when they were finished. When the tiles were fitted into place a week or so later, the mission had a solid, well-roofed church that water could not enter to fall upon the altar and its sacred vessels or on the heads of the men and women who came to pray.

The season was now at hand when the weather and the condition of the clay-like soil demanded the planting of the winter wheat, this time over an area much more extensive than ever before. The construction crews put away their axes, saws, hammers, and measuring sticks and took up instead their plows, hoes, shovels, and seed.

Ixtil loved this work far better than the erection of buildings. Mists clung to the summit and sides of Mt. San Luis; the air was fresh and smelled of the rain which from time to time drifted down lightly on his face; the hills and meadows were turning green; the rivers ran high and fierce with the floods that fed them in the hills. How great were the creations of *el Dios bueno!* And all because he loved the tribes of men.

Ixtil found himself humming the "Alabado," which was like a praise of the Holy Family set to music:

> Praised and worshiped be
> The Divine Sacrament, in which God;
> Hidden, helps to nourish souls.

> Praised also be the Immaculate Conception
> Of Mary, Queen of Heaven,
> Who, remaining a pure Virgin,
> Is the Mother of the eternal Word.

> Praised, too be Blessed Saint Joseph,
> Chosen by God Almighty
> As worthy to be the foster-father
> Of His Son, the Divine Word.

> This Son is for all the ages to come
> And from all the ages past. Amen.
> Amen, Jesus and Mary,
> Jesus, Mary, and Joseph!

It had a nobility, that song, and was not to be taken lightly or prayed on every casual occasion. Also, sadness mixed with gladness in it, as Fr. Joseph was teaching the choir, of which Ixtil was a diligent member. Perhaps because human life is both sad and glad, as he was learning to live it.

The planting of wheat being finished and that of beans, peas, potatoes, and corn still to come, preparations went forward for the great Christmas fiestas. Most of all, Ixtil liked the staging of *Las Posadas* on Christmas Eve, which showed how the Blessed Virgin could not find a room in which to rest herself, though the stern Joseph knocked loudly on the doors of all the inns of Bethlehem demanding one. Therefore the Son of God had to be born in a cave where oxen were kept, eating the hay. *Ai, ai, ai;* no wonder the baby Jesus cried, like all who are born into this world of pain. Besides, Jesus came all alone to save it, without saints and angels to help him.

During Christmas Mass at midnight, Ixtil, sitting with the choir, tried to put these feelings into the notes of his flute from the tree of music, while he gave a steady beat to the singing. The three priests, in their stately red and gold vestments, chanted the Latin words at the altar. With the censers, they spread the incense sweetly throughout the church. They made the necessary genuflections. Then, at last, Fr. Joseph held up the body and blood of the divine Jesus for all to see and understand, if only they tried. Everyone in the crowded church received a little crumb of the Host, first the women, standing together on one side of the aisle, then the men from the other side.

At midnight, the church rang all its bells and everybody cheered, for now it was the day on which Jesus was born many centuries ago.

Naturally, there could be no work on Christmas

Day. The people slept late and, when they woke up they put on their best clothes and went visiting one another. Ixtil and Ysaga had intended to do the same, but it had become known to all that the young couple had received from the priests, as a reward for Ixtil's ride to Mission San Antonio a big piece of chocolate and a roast from a cow which had been slain on purpose. So they had relatives, friends, and even mere acquaintances coming and eating all day long, until the gifts were totally consumed.

This struck Ixtil and Ysaga as a great joke upon themselves. When the last visitors had departed with the last bit of chocolate, they fell into each other's arms laughing, until the laughter wearied them.

"Next year," Ysaga said, drying her eyes, "we must leave the house much earlier, before anybody comes."

"Or stay in the church all night and not come home at all?" Ixtil suggested.

This set them laughing again. It was a good Christmas.

Chapter 10

After the holiday, the usual things happened. Rains fell, but never quite as much as some people wanted. Not enough children were born, and too many adults died, and not only the old ones. The other crops were put into the earth as the season and the soil dictated. Ysaga helped in the *monjerio,* but chiefly waited quietly at home for her baby to come.

Ixtil waited too, but with less intensity. He was busy in the mornings with catechism classes, entrusted to him by Fr. Joseph. He taught them in both Chumash and Spanish, and tried to reach his pupils souls with the truths he was teaching. At other times he was needed to help in agriculture, or in the branding of cattle, or in the care of newly born calves. But the newborn colts brought him most delight. He looked after the mares and colts when they were sick. He curried them all repeatedly and well, and made sure that each got enough to eat.

But on the third day of the month called March, in the year belonging to God, 1776, the loud, continued clanging of the mission bells told Ixtil, who was in the stables, that some visitor or other had been sighted in the valley, coming up from the south. After hurrying his work Ixtil ran to the front of the church, where all three priests were assembling in festive robes to greet those who were arriving.

One glance showed him that these were no ordinary visitors. In a long procession, walking and riding, were some 200 people, counting all the soldiers, and all the women and children he could see in the dust they raised. After the people paced whole herds of cattle, followed by hundreds of horses and pack mules, all bearing burdens. Later, he counted the number of the cattle to be 325 and of horses and mules 695. And who should be riding a big roan stallion at the head of the column but *Señor* De Anza, next to the soldier displaying the flag of the King on the tip of his lance!

"I'm back!" he roared to everybody. He gave the *abrazo* to each of the priests and impartially to the men he recognized in the crowd cheering him. When he came to the spot where Ixtil waited in the ranks of his admirers, De Anza called, *"Hola!* You too, *amigo,* not the least of those I love." Grasping Ixtil to him, he kissed both cheeks. "I hear you found your Ysaga and are married now. She is well?"

"With child, *señor*."

"What else? You were ever a man of action. I shall want to hear the whole story during or after the *comida.* Know also my *teniente,* Pablo Moraga, and my chaplain, Fr. Pedro Font, a great student of maps, enough to weary anybody else."

Immediately, Ixtil liked Moraga, a bold-looking young man with an open countenance and keen blue eyes. Fr. Font had evidently studied too many maps, for he wore glasses over his eyes. A conscientious priest, however, Ixtil judged.

The mission had not enough food ready to feed such a multitude, but the resident women busied themselves with the wheat to cook at least some thin bread for the guests. By families, these guests encamped themselves over the grassy plain in front of the church. Ixtil and Ysaga went among them to bestow the bread and to exchange with each family a welcome spoken in the tongue of Spain. These people, Ixtil learned, had left Mexico for good in order to become settlers of bounteous California.

"It was a hard decision for us women," one wife told him and Ysaga, "to leave our homes, taking only what would rest on the backs of two mules. What a leaving behind, alas! But my man wanted to come as a soldier, and the Captain said he would take only *hombres de familia*. Also, the children will benefit here, we hope. I am Isabel."

While Ysaga talked with Isabel, Ixtil viewed the youngsters who were dashing about from one campfire to another like schools of fingerlings, but more noisily. Might these children one day replace us Chumash, he wondered. Only if they can outbreed us. Meanwhile, they were imps of activity whom he enjoyed watching. He had never seen so many children playing at once.

Whether because of her cooking and walking or some instinct of her body, Ysaga's baby gave her the first pains that day. Ixtil nervously half carried, half walked her back to the mission and directly to the hospital. First he sent for Fr. Joseph. Then he trotted to their cabin and brought the mattress for her to lie on. Remembering his sister's death in this very place, he knelt for what seemed like hours, until Fr. Joseph arrived, and after that for more hours, until the baby decided to come out safely. It cried at first, being a healthy boy, until Ysaga gave him her breast, where he sucked lustily. Nevertheless, Fr. Joseph prepared to baptize him immediately.

A heavy step and a massive shadow announced the coming of De Anza. "I heard that the little one was being born. Forgive me if I intrude. *Con permiso,* I would be honored to stand as the boy's godfather."

Ixtil looked at Ysaga, who nodded. "The honor is greatly ours, *Señor Capitan,*" he told De Anza.

"What name have you chosen for him, *chiquita*?"

"Francisco Maria for God. But we will call him Ponce for ourselves."

The priest baptized the child by that name, as all said the necessary words.

"I will sleep now, I think," Ysaga said, gathering her baby close.

"Fr. Joseph," said De Anza, "you and I have interrupted our *comida* in the middle, and Ixtil has had none at all. Let's go back to the table." While they ate, Ixtil asked the Captain how he had managed to assemble so large an expedition. De Anza laughed in his beard.

"When the good Viceroy Bucareli and his Council heard that I had opened a land route from Mexico to California, they decided, even before I reached home, that they wanted not only to explore California and build *presidios* to fortify it, and missions to Christianize it, but also to establish towns to populate it with Spanish and Mexican settlers. Of course, I was their golden boy. So who else but De Anza should be given the power—and the money, I might add—to select only soldiers with wives and children, only farmers thoroughly married and childed, only artisans similarly well bound by families, and so on? Everybody married, and the more children the better."

He laughed heartily. "I, De Anza, with never a wife or child, to lead all those *maridos!* Ah, *la vida!* Full of ironies."

He paused to drink. "All the animals too are paired, male with female. Cows with bulls, mares with stallions, hens with roosters. But the mules, the burden bearers who can have no offspring, and I, *simpatico* with them, we came alone." He stopped for a sigh and went on without laughter. "The *maridos* cannot do without us. We have marched aboard the ark with the rest."

Fr. Joseph asked, "Where are the settlements to be? Can you pick your own locations?"

De Anza frowned. "That, Father, was left beautifully unclear. Or at least I thought it was beautiful, until I met Governor Rivera. My instructions from the Viceroy are to establish a *presidio* at the tip of the peninsula in the Bay of San Francisco. And also—here enters the unclearness—to inspect the peninsula for good sites for missions. Merely to find the sites, or also to take the priests to found the missions there? What is the Governor's usual function in founding missions, Fr. Joseph?"

Fr. Joseph considered. "The custom has always been that the Viceroy chooses the general region where a mission is to be set up. But the specific site within that region is selected by us priests, usually by Fr. Serra as *Padre Presidente* of the California missions, and usually after consulting the Governor. You observe, *Señor,*" said Fr. Joseph with a smile, "that our practice is at least as ambiguous as your instructions."

"But what, then, of my settlers?" De Anza demanded impatiently. "Does custom give me the right to place them in *pueblos* wherever I believe they are most likely to prosper?"

Fr. Cavaller spoke with great care, choosing his words well.

"You ask me to walk on dangerous ground, *Señor*. On this point we have little custom and many opinions. So far, we have in Alta California only two pueblos for Spaniards, *gente de razon* we call them. One is at San Diego, the other at Monterey. Both of these are near both a *presidio* and a mission, where Spanish guns protect their trade with each other and with foreign ships sailing along our coast.

"Some say that this is ideal, that a mission, a pueblo, and a presidio form a perfect trinity. Fr.

Serra, however, believes that the proximity of either a pueblo or a presidio spoils the teaching of religion at a mission, and that the mission in turn tempts the people of the *pueblo* to take advantage of the mission *Indios* in ways not conducive to morality. I am inclined to agree with him."

De Anza mulled these ideas over in a long silence.

"I think," he decided at last, "that I should yield to Governor Rivera in the matter of choosing sites for missions. But he must certainly yield to me in the founding of *presidios* and *pueblos*. May God make him an easier man to deal with!"

"You have spoken with him, Sir?" Ixtil asked, wondering whether De Anza's dislike for the Governor was as great as his own.

"Yes, at Mission San Diego, which the *Indios* of the region attacked some weeks ago, killing one of the priests. Leaving most of my people at Mission San Gabriel, which I had just reached after crossing the desert to the east, I hurried there with a small band of my best fighters to assist the Governor in quelling the rebellion. He could not make up his mind what to do!

"When I suggested pursuing the attackers into the back country, he was too timid to go with me. He spent his hours drawing up one plan of action after another—and acting on none. He was still debating with himself what to do when I became sick of waiting about and returned to San Gabriel to bring my settlers north. I was never so glad to leave a place, or a man."

This was a new Rivera to Ixtil, so he said nothing; but De Anza was looking straight across the table at him.

"I would like to have you with me again, Ixtil, if you wish to come, and if Fr. Joseph permits."

Ixtil thought of Ysaga, lying asleep in the hospital with her arm around little Ponce.

"I could not come for several days, until I became sure that all is well with my wife and son, *Señor Commandante,* and by that time you will be many miles away. Otherwise I would delight to go with you."

De Anza got up from his chair, stretching himself like a cat. "Come, Ixtil. Let us walk about and see what the mission is doing. Sitting still too long bores me."

Outside, as they strolled, he said, "I shall leave a fast horse here for you in case you decide to join me."

Ixtil expressed his thanks and led De Anza unobtrusively in the direction of the hospital.

The Spanish leader laughed. "I know where you are taking me. Why not head straight for the hospital?" They found Ysaga awake and nursing her baby. "He is always hungary, this one," she said with pride. "It is good to feel life in my arms, for next door I can hear a woman dying. Fr. Joseph has just arrived to help her."

They stayed with Ysaga until the cries next door ended, and they heard the murmur of prayers. Presently, Fr. Joseph came in with a cheery word for Ysaga.

Outside, as they strolled, he said, "I shall leave to Ixtil. "The same disease of the female organs which killed your sister. How many more will die?"

"My advice, Father," De Anza said, "is to bury her quickly and, so far as possible, without anyone touching her body, especially the sores. I could not help noticing how rapidly your *campo santo* is filling up."

"It fills as God wills," the priest said sadly.

"No doubt," De Anza answered gently, "but *el*

Dios bueno wishes you first to try every means to drive the disease away and to prevent its spreading. In case you do not know, it passes between men and women who lie together, and it has no cure whatever. It lasts long, sometimes for many years, but it always kills in the end. Since it cannot be cured, the only safety lies in keeping the sick ones from intercourse with those who are well."

"But who can tell who the sick ones are?" Fr. Joseph asked anxiously.

"You, or anybody with eyes, who can persuade men and women to let themselves be examined. Since this sickness passes from one to another by touch, all who identify or treat the sick must keep themselves clean by washing often and thoroughly. Let me tell you what I did with those who wished to come to California with me."

De Anza smiled ferociously. "No doctor, I, but with my own eyes I searched every person—man, woman, or child. Yes, I, De Anza, often got down on my knees to look more closely." He laughed. "I was a funny sight. Those who watched told me that I resembled a small boy preparing to be spanked. But I persevered, rejecting those whose condition did not please me. The result: All my settlers are healthy— I think."

"We cannot reject anybody here," Ixtil objected. "Where could they go?"

De Anza spoke grimly. "Into a region called "quarantine." Tell all the healthy ones who the sick ones are, and warn of the consequences of the disease. Order them to leave the sick people strictly alone, not even to touch them. A few will disobey, and die. Most will obey, through fright, and live. Let the single women beware especially of soldiers, who are often infected secretly."

"What is it called, this evil thing?"

"The pox," said De Anza. "The French call it the Spanish pox, and we call it the Italian pox, brought back from the New World by Columbus, who was of Genoa. And the Italians name it the French pox. A perfect circle, you see." De Anza paused to chuckle.

"Every nation is anxious to credit some other nation with its origins. Myself, I think it has always existed, under other names, since Adam and Eve sinned and God smote them." He crossed himself. "May He not smite me!

"Having this disease disposes its possessor to all other diseases—of the lungs, the throat, the eyes, the stomach. Consequently, the pox is often the first cause of death and the other diseases often only the second."

"Most terrible!" Ixtil exclaimed, thinking of the dangers besetting his little family.

"Sad and terrible indeed," said Fr. Joseph, thinking of his converts.

Next day, Ysaga and little Ponce left the hospital and went back to the hut under the live oak, where they prospered so well that, four days later, Ixtil felt safe in leaving them in the care of Fr. Joseph and an old Chumash woman who lived next door.

De Anza had left his big roan, Rojo, for Ixtil, a singular mark of favor. On him Ixtil set out for Monterey at a moderate pace, not racing as when he brought the bread and wine from Mission San Antonio. This time he was able to enjoy much more the beauty of the green hills rising up to a pale blue sky without clouds, and the meadows so adorned with masses of lupin, poppies, daisies of many hues, and roses of Castile. He was dazzled by these works of *el Dios bueno.* Their beauty entered deep into his soul and made a garden there.

At Mission San Antonio, Fr. Sitjar and Fr. Pieras

not only gave him the hospitality of food and wine, as is the way in missions, but treated him as an old friend. He told them the story of the Week of the Tiles, of which they wished to hear every part.

"Captain De Anza's multitude passed through here two days ago," Fr. Pieras informed him when he had ended. "At the rate he was covering the distances, he must be in Monterey by now. You will not catch that man."

"Having ridden with him once, I do not try," said Ixtil, and they laughed together. When he left, the priests' blessing made him feel clean.

De Anza was preparing to leave Monterey for the north in two or three days, Ixtil learned when inquiring of his whereabouts. He rode toward the *pueblo* with his eyes wide with wonder. Inside the *presidio* stockade, he encountered several solid buildings—not tule huts—made from timber cut in the woods of pine growing all around. At the Governor's house, he was hailed by De Anza.

"Welcome to Monterey, Ixtil! I take it that Ysaga and the baby are well? Good. You remember that I told you Governor Rivera is still in San Diego? Consequently, I have moved into his half-timbered mansion. How lucky for me, in all sorts of ways, that he is not here."

Ixtil saw that De Anza was in one of his mischievous moods and returned his greeting with zest.

"We leave for San Francisco Bay day after tomorrow," Spain's fastest Captain told him. "Come, help me check the lists of supplies."

In one of the large storerooms attached to the Governor's dwelling, orderly stacks of supplies lay on the floor, heap after heap: powder and musket balls, muskets leaning in lines along the walls, a variety of imperishable foods, grain for the horses, saddles, ropes, bridles and bits, blankets and heavy coats, and many items for which Ixtil could scarcely imagine a need. De Anza called out the kinds and quantities while Ixtil checked them off on a long roll of paper.

"We go to the North Pole, *Señor?*" Ixtil asked as he surveyed the room.

"Only as far as the Bay of San Francisco, humorist, but you will see how little of this will be unconsumed when we return, say in two weeks. And only sixteen of us are to go. Twelve troopers; my friend and second in command, Lt. Moraga; Fr. Font, with his diaries and maps; you, with your abilities to read and write Spanish, and possibly to understand the tongue of the *Indios* of that region; and myself. My settlers we shall leave dangling here, camped among the pinewoods. But we shall be looking sharp for favorable spots where they may build their *pueblos* up and down the peninsula of San Francisco.

"I suggest you spend some hours with Fr. Font this afternoon. Tomorrow you may want to visit the Mission San Carlos, newly relocated at the Rio del Carmelo, over those hills behind the house."

"What priests are there, Sir?"

"Fr. Serra and—let me think. When Fr. Serra is somewhere, who can remember what others are with him?"

Ixtil thanked him and left to find Fr. Font, who, he discovered, had made for himself a brushwood shelter. Over the head of the bed hung a painting of the Virgen de Gaudalupe, who had appeared near Mexico City to the poor peasant, Juan, in the year belonging to God, 1531, and had thereby converted, at one stroke, all the *Indios* of Mexico. Truly a great miracle. Ixtil knew well the Spanish statues and pictures of Nuestra Señora del Pilar, suffering with her divine Son when he was scourged by the soldiers of Rome at the pillar of Pilate's palace. But how the Mother of God looked when she spoke at Guadalupe he had not known at all.

Fr. Font saw Ixtil examining the painting. "She is not like the Virgen del Pilar prayed to by the Spaniards, is she?"

"She resembles the *Indios* of Mexico, perhaps?"

"She does indeed. In her divine courtesy she has changed herself to resemble us of Mexico. In that blessed form she intercedes for us with her Son." He crossed himself with exactitude, worship in his eyes.

Ixtil said in wonder, "Father, you speak Spanish. Yet you are not of Spain, like the other priests?"

"No, I am of Mexico, born on her soil. The Spanish priests have their House of San Fernando, in Ciudad de Mexico. We Mexicans have ours at Querétaro."

"Yet all are equally of the Order of Franciscans?"

"Equally. Any man who has a vocation to be a priest can become a Franciscan, after study and examination. Mexicans, Spaniards, Italians, French—men of all countries in the world may become members of the order. We are worldwide."

Ixtil stood in silence contemplating those facts. He saw that the Church of *el Cristo bueno* and His Mother was much larger, much, much deeper, than the little gods of the Chumash. He felt almost sorry for Sup.

"Come," said the priest, "I observe that you are a thoughtful young man. Let me show you my little library of diaries, and the maps made from them, which are most precious to me—next to that painting of Nuestra Señora de Guadalupe." From his leather-covered chest, which also housed the necessities for saying Mass, he drew some thin, closely written books.

"These," he said proudly, "are copies of the diaries made by all the priests who have accompanied the land explorers of California. Here is Fr. Juan Crespi's journal of the Portolá expeditions, *anno Domini* 1769 and 1770. Here also is his journal of the expedition up the east side of the Bay of San Francisco in March 1772. Of that journal, now in the archives of the Viceroy in Ciudad de Mexico, my brother Pablo has sent me this copy. Also, here is Fr. Palóu's account of the peninsula on the west side of the bay, where we are going." Fr. Font laid them aside carefully.

"Attached to every journal is a map of the land-marks of the region. The maps are rolled up, and must be unrolled—like this—and laid on a flat surface for perusal." He unrolled the Palóu map of his penin-sula trip and spread it on a table, weighing down the corners with washed stones.

"Study it well. This outlines the country to which *Señor* De Anza is taking us. But it is crude and marred by guesses. Fr. Palóu did not have the time to go where he willed. I expect to improve it. Sit at the table and study it as long as you desire."

To Ixtil, sitting and memorizing it inch by inch, it did not seem at all crude, but he reflected that he did not know the way of maps and their makers as Fr. Font did. That man was a true scholar of maps, who must be respected. When Ixtil had printed it all on his brain and briefly handled the other maps, he thanked the learned priest and took his leave, He had much to ponder during the evening.

A cold March wind from the sea ruffled the waters of Monterey Bay and roared through the pines as he walked over the hills to Mission San Carlos Borromeo at Carmel early next morning. This was a foggy place, this Monterey Bay. Ixtil did not think he would like to live here. Nor did the mission seem to him much better sheltered. It stood on high ground overlooking a warm, fertile valley through which a river meandered on its way to the ocean. Behind the mission and downward, the rough sea continued its everlasting onslaught against the land. At a distance, through fog and spray, he could discern the outlines of the craggy headland called Los Lobos because the wolves of the sea barked there in great numbers.

At the mission, the Indians did not understand his Chumash nor did he understand their language. They could converse only in Spanish, of which these Indians knew less than the people of his own Mission San Luis Obispo. Finally, they took him into a building to Fr. Serra, who rose from his writing to greet him.

"Welcome! Welcome, Ixtil!" said the famous *Presidente* of all the priests with his usual intensity of manner. "We shall speak in Spanish. I am still trying to master the speech of my converts here, with indifferent success. For me to try to talk to you in Chumash would be presumptuous." He smiled ruefully. "I understand that you are to accompany De Anza as a kind of secretary and interpreter. Would that I had one like you here."

To Ixtil, this sounded like an invitation he had better decline right away. "Were I not so concerned about my wife and our new baby," he said, "and about the people of my tribe at my mission, it would be an honor to serve you, *Padre Presidente.*"

"No, no, you must stay with them, of course!" Fr. Serra exclaimed.

He gestured with distaste at the papers piled high on the table he used as his desk.

"You little know what you would be letting yourself in for, my son, as a secretary of mine. In this pile, for instance, are questions from my religious superiors at the House of San Fernando in Mexico City about the progress each mission—*each* mission—is making in bringing the tribes to Christ. Here, correspondence with Governor Rivera about the scarcity of his soldiers and the superabundant number of missions which they must guard. He resents every new mission to be founded, including the two being planned for the area of San Francisco Bay. He and his troops want a fixed share of the food produced by the missions. And as for correspondence with Viceroy Bucareli—he is almost too solicitous for our welfare."

Fr. Serra sighed with exasperation. "I am a priest—first, last, and always—not an administrator. Yet I find myself imprisoned most of the day in this office of mine, and all these documents are the bars."

"Padre Presidente," Ixtil said, "I am free for the remainder of the day. If you wish to dictate some of these letters quite slowly, I could write them down for you."

In this way Fr. Serra completed his answers to the Viceroy and to the House of San Fernando that afternoon.

"Thank you, Ixtil, for saving me many hours of labor," he said. "Well, sufficient unto the day. . . It is time for supper, which you must share with us. I insist."

The meal was Spartan indeed, but Fr. Serra's prayers before and after transformed it into a feast. Ixtil walked back to Monterey in the dusk with a deep sense of accomplishment. And knowing that De Anza always started his journeys at dawn, he went straight to bed.

Chapter 11

Riding imperiously at the head of his band of twelve troopers, with Lt. Moraga carrying the King's banner at his side, De Anza led them forth at first light. Fr. Font and Ixtil brought up the rear, which they deemed their place. De Anza set a speed which made all talk impossible. The column maintained that order during the days that followed, until De Anza caught his first glimpse of the southernmost waters of the bay, flashing in the sunlight.

Fr. Font and his pupil, Ixtil, then received the summons to come forward. A short session with Fr. Font's maps decided their leader that their best route up the peninsula lay along the eastern foot of the hills that separate the valley from the ocean to the west. The western side of the hills, already surveyed by the Portolá expedition, offered no suitable sites for a *presidio* or a *pueblo,* which were De Anza's chief objects.

All that day the party rode northward up the peninsula through a most fertile valley, where the white oaks grew to such size and spread their heavy arms so wide that many of their branches had broken off and lay in ruins where they fell. Huge live oaks shaded out almost all undergrowth. The salt smell of the sea grew sharper. At length, on the fifth day after leaving Monterey, they halted at the peninsula's northernmost point.

The cliffs on which they stood rose straight up out of

a gray arm of the ocean, an entrance to the bay, about a mile wide at that point. On the other side, wooded hills bounded the shore. Ixtil saw that the waters between were anything but calm and navigable. The tides were pouring in from the ocean with a prodigious flow, bringing with them the vast salt breathing of the sea. On their surface, flotsam raced past. Ixtil thought he would not like to try crossing it in a Chumash canoe. To his right, the shoreline extended several miles, gradually curving southward out of sight, to form, he guessed, the peninsula's eastern side.

"Bring the Ayala map, Fr. Font," De Anza commanded.

Ixtil was not close enough to hear what the two men said in their conference, but it ended in De Anza's saying aloud with satisfaction, "Yes, this is the spot. Thank you." He then addressed his men.

"To our good fortune, Captain Ayala last year sailed his ship from the open ocean through the narrow gap you see in front of you and into every inlet of this great bay, no doubt the greatest in the world. In fact, he was the first man to prove that it is a bay. For many years the captains of the annual Philippine galleon have deceived us, and themselves, by calling a shallow curving inlet, some miles north of where we stand, by the name of *La Bahia de San Francisco.* And ever since Captain Portolá first reached here in 1769, we Spaniards have been trying vainly to cross the gap of water in front of you in order to reach that false *bahia.*" He shook his head, laughing.

"Now all that is over. The true Bay of San Francisco opens itself before you. It is landlocked, protected from winds and storms. Many miles of its shores are suitable for anchorage. Whoever controls it will dominate the whole of northern California in the future. And our *presidio,* to be established here, will block the

Russians from pressing southward."

Musing, he sat silent on his horse for a minute before continuing.

"The narrow entrance you see before you is the bay's only opening to the sea. The cannon from our *presidio* will command the gateway to the bay. We of Spain will command the *presidio,* the *presidio* will command the bay, and the bay will control the country north and south of here in all directions. Therefore, comrades, this is the strategic location for our *presidio.* Plant the flag, Lt. Moraga!"

Ixtil had been wondering why the gleaming lance on which the lieutenant carried the flag had a sharp tip at the bottom end, and now he saw why. Moraga backed his horse a long distance from the spot designated by De Anza. Then, at full gallop, he rode toward it and, as he did so, flung the lance skyward with a mighty heave. It flew in a high arc, the flag streaming out behind it, then fell, and its point stuck quivering in the earth. At its upper tip the lions and castles of the Spanish King flapped in the sea wind. The men cheered.

In turn, De Anza backed off his big roan. He, too, spurred it to fiery speed but, as he neared the flag, he leaned far down and snatched a lump of earth as he passed. With a shout he hurled it into the teeth of the west wind. Three times more he repeated the ceremony, throwing the soil to east, north, and south. Having done so, he curbed his horse next to the flag and shouted in his great voice.

"I, Juan Bautista de Anza, take possession of this territory in the name of my King, *Carlos Secundo, el Rey de Leon y Castilio.*" His shout, reinforced by the cheers of his men, seemed to float over the whole bay and possess it.

Then solemnly, doffing his helmet, De Anza said,

"Amigos, let us not forget the God who has made this possible. Fr. Font, please lead us in the *'Alabado.'"*

In the solitude, the song rang out—sung by Spaniards from time immemorial, in tempests and safe landfalls, in triumph and disaster, praising Jesus, Mary, and Joseph for all the centuries to come. To this declaration of faith, Ixtil added his voice, as he had to the cheers before it. At that moment he was proud to be a sort of Spaniard, even at several removes.

That afternoon, De Anza paced off the boundaries of the *presidio,* setting up piles of stones at the corners and at intervals along its lines of length and breadth. He had expressed concern at the lack of an all-season water supply; however, Ixtil had done some scouting with that in mind. He showed the Captain, at a distance of somewhat less than a mile to the east, an *arroyo* through which ran a plentiful stream on its way to form a lake in the hollow of the surrounding hills.

As he led his men in the morning, De Anza stopped them and said, pointing to the lake, "This water shall be called *Nuestra Señora de los Dolores,* in honor of Our Lady's tears at the crucifixion of her Son." Fr. Font entered the name in his diary.

De Anza resumed, "Lazy people have a way of taking the soul out of a name in order to say it faster. So, Father, underline that its name dedicates it to *Nuestra Señora,* lest in times to come men with more haste than religion reduce it to *Dolores,* which by itself means mothing."

Fr. Font did so, remarking, "I shall also write the comment that a mission on this lake's shore would be happily situated. The *presidio* troops would protect it, and the *Indios* could help the *presidio* in many ways."

"True," said De Anza with a laugh, "but mind you

do not attribute the idea to me, or Governor Rivera will have my head. I promised him that we would take note of possible sites for missions, but not found any. *Adelante!*"

On the way back, they hugged the eastern shore of the peninsula because they had come by the westerly side and knew that way already. Fr. Font kept stopping so often to draw his map of their route, and was so entranced with several locations for missions on the banks of streams halfway down the peninsula, that De Anza's patience, never very durable, gave way altogether more than once.

"*Por Dios, Padre!* Come along or we may lose you. Do you think that anyone will wish to start a foundation here, only ten to fifteen miles from Mission San Francisco de Asís? Put away those mission maps until I tell you. Look for a site for another *pueblo,* not for another mission! That is the order the Viceroy gave me."

Fr. Font would shrug and try to roll up his multitudinous maps and diaries neatly, but they had a wicked tendency to slide out of his grasp and entangle themselves with one another.

"I am discovering that there is a practical limit to the number of documents one can bring on a trip of this sort, especially where its commander is so impatient," the priest admitted to Ixtil on one such occasion. "Good God, why did I have the folly to bring all these along in an expedition led by De Anza?"

At the peninsula's southernmost end, the party was surprised to encounter a river flowing into the bay. No map showed this *rio,* although it carried a considerable volume of clear water. Fr. Font carefully traced it on his map.

"*Señor Commandante,*" he ventured to say to De

Anza, "here in these meadows, close to this *rio,* a
mission would prosper, or a *pueblo,* or perhaps both
together. We have come at least thirty miles from the
presidio, with its Mission San Francisco de Asís presumably in or near it."

"Agreed," said De Anza, gazing with favor on the
resources of the scene around him. "What will you
name the *rio*?"

"Con permiso, after our Virgin of Mexico," Fr.
Font declared. "I shall dedicate the *rio* and its adjoin-
ing meadows to the patronage of *Nuestra Señora de
Guadalupe."*

De Anza nodded. "It shall be so. At whatever places
she makes herself visible, whether in Spain or New
Spain, she is always the one Virgin. Is it not so?"

"It is so, Excellency, although she had a special
reason for appearing to Juan Diego, the Indio, at
Guadalupe. Through him she converted an entire
race, newly humbled and enslaved by conquest, to a
belief in her Son and His Church."

De Anza crossed himself devoutly. "You humble
me, Father, for the good of my soul. If I return
safely to Mexico I shall pray a novena in her praise."
In an abrupt change of mood he shouted for his
lieutenant. *"Hola,* Moraga!"

When Moraga rode up, De Anza told him: "Take
note, *Teniente,* that I favor a mission somewhere
along this *rio,* but I do not *specify* a particular site,
as agreed with Governor Rivera. Viceroy Bucareli
has finally made up his mind that since San Francisco
de Asís and Santa Clara, of the same city, were
helpmates while they lived, their missions should ad-
join each other on this peninsula. Now, Mission San
Francisco will rise in or near the *presidio.* So, Mission
Santa Clara should arise somewhere down here, possibly on this fine *rio.*

"Another thing. My commission authorizes me to start two new *pueblos* in this region. One, by my choice, is to grow around the *presidio*. That is fixed. The second *pueblo* must be here, somewhere, divided from Mission Santa Clara by this *rio*. By my authority you will found it after both the *presidio* and Mission San Francisco de Asís have been built. You will call this *pueblo* San José de Guadalupe. You will fix its exact location after negotiation with the priests of Mission Santa Clara. Understood?"

"Yes, Captain," his lieutenant replied, "all except the reason why you will not accomplish all these actions yourself."

De Anza put his arm around the younger man's shoulders. "Because, Lieutenant, I shall be returning soon to Mexico City, and perhaps even to Madrid, if summoned by our King and his Council of the Indies. Never grieve, my faithful one. Without my overbearing presence you will all the sooner become the authoritative man you are capable of becoming. Now, please, call the men together."

When they were gathered, De Anza told them that he was going to take them for a brief look at the east side of the bay, opposite the peninsula. "Several expeditions like ours have followed that shore and discovered nothing. But you know me, *amigos*. I do not accept what other men report. I prefer to look with my own eyes, and yours. If we limit that journey to about fifty miles, we should still be able to enter Monterey, where letters await me, by April 8 or so."

For two days they rode up the east side and only once did they stop during the daytime. De Anza paused long at the mouth of a valley that ran far upward into the mountains. He even rode a few miles into it and looked about thoughtfully. On his return

he told Moraga, in Ixtil's presence, "This seems to be
a pass through the coast range, much used by *Indios,*
to judge from their signs. If the tribes to the interior
are warlike, as they usually are, it would be wise to
close the pass with a *presidio,* or even a well-guarded
mission, or perhaps both."

He beckoned Ixtil closer. "Have you been able to
find *Indios* of this region to talk with? Do they provide
any useful information about this problem?"

Ixtil marshaled his thoughts. "Not to talk to, exactly. The *Indios* who live near the *presidio* are poor
creatures and few, because of the cold and damp.
More energetic and quite numerous are the tribes
near the Rio Guadalupe, as you no doubt observed.
But except for a few similarities here and there, our
languages are so strange to each other that we can
exchange little except by signs. They do not yet speak
Spanish either. I gather that the *Indios* inland are
indeed fierce. They sometimes erupt from these mountains to rob and slay. The coastal tribes will welcome
a *pueblo,* a mission, a *presidio*—anything that would
help them, even by distracting the attention of their
enemies."

"As I feared, we shall have to pay in blood to
command this bay," De Anza said moodily, "and we
have little of that commodity to spare." Thereafter
he rode for long distances in silence.

Arriving in Monterey near the date he had forecast,
De Anza called immediately for his mail. He leafed
through it rapidly, then threw it violently on the
table. "Nothing from the courageous Governor Rivera!"
he exclaimed with disgust. "Can the man still be
dallying in San Diego, undecided what to do about
the Indian uprising? Before I left for the peninsula I
wrote to him by express carrier outlining my intentions.
That was nearly three weeks ago. Has he no comment,

no approval or objection—nothing at all?"

He strode the floor angrily. "I must send a note to Fr. Serra, asking whether he has fared better, perhaps."

Fr. Serra brought his answer personally, riding on a soft-paced burro which respected his lame leg, and De Anza and Ixtil knelt for his blessing.

"Ah," he said, alighting, "you make quite a pair, you two: one mighty in mind and body, the other growing ever richer in spirit. What is it that troubles you, *Señor?*"

"Come, let us sit inside, out of this vile wind," De Anza said. When they were comfortably settled, he asked Fr. Serra whether he had any mail from San Diego that concerned the movements of Governor Rivera.

"Yes, and none of it good." The *padre* sighed. "Fr. Lasuén writes that one of the Indians who led the assault on the mission took sanctuary at the altar. The three priests in charge conferred and decided that the fugitive could not be arrested so long as he clung to the large crucifix hanging above it. That is in accord with canon law, *Señor,* and must be obeyed.

"Well, after a day or two, Governor Rivera ordered the priests to bring the rebel out of the church, where he might be arrested. This they properly refused to do."

Ixtil could not restrain himself. "What if the Governor had not commanded the priests but had calmly persuaded them to try to bring the man from the sanctuary peaceably, maybe with a safe-conduct to return to his tribe in the hills?"

Fr. Serra weighed Ixtil with a glance and smiled. "In that case, much grief for all concerned would have been avoided, Ixtil. Blessed are the peacemakers, and you are one. But Governor Rivera does not persuade: He orders. His next move was to appear in the church with a squad of soldiers and order them to drag the *Indio* from his sanctuary by force. Fr. Lasuén then publicly excommunicated the Governor, with an offer to remove the ban if he would restore his captive to sanctuary. The offer was just a few minutes too late. Rivera had already hanged the man."

"So Rivera still bears the ban?" asked De Anza.

"Yes, indeed, *Señor,* until his case is heard by a tribunal in Mexico City," the *Padre Presidente* declared emphatically. His mouth worked as if tasting bitter fruit. "I pity everyone who was enmeshed in this tragedy: the *Indio,* who wished to be pardoned and to live; my priests, who had to obey the canon law; the Governor's soldiers, who, though troubled in their minds, obeyed his commands, as was their duty; and most of all Governor Rivera himself, who acted as he believed a Governor should, for the peace of his province."

"Where is he now, Father?" De Anza asked.

"Somewhere on El Camino, riding north to Monterey, and in a vile humor, I'm told."

De Anza spoke thoughtfully. "I do not think that, after all this, such an inept man will long retain his post as Governor. What is best for me to do? Let me think." He sat pondering, then smashed his fist on the table.

"Two things. One, I must convince him that on my expedition up the peninsula I have chosen only sites for a *presidio* and two *pueblos,* as required of me by the Viceroy, but definitely not sites for any missions, though I took note of favorable places for them. If he approves of what I have done, he must agree to let Lt. Moraga press ahead with the founding of the *presidio* and the *pueblos.* Selecting sites for missions, and the founding of them, I freely acknowledge to be the prerogative of the Governor and of your priests,

Padre Presidente.

"But what if he does not agree to permit construction of the *presidio* and the *pueblos?* Then I will leave instructions with Lt. Moraga to found them anyway.

"The other thing I must do, with reluctance, is ride to meet Rivera on El Camino to straighten out the terms of our agreement. If he refuses to acknowledge my authority to build the *presidio* and the *pueblos,* I must lure him southward with me by prolonging the negotiations, so as to win the time Moraga needs to prepare the soldiers and settlers I brought here for their trek to the peninsula."

"A devious scheme, *Señor,*" Fr. Serra commented. "I do not like the luring and the secrecy."

He walked to the doorway, fingering his rosary, and stood looking over Monterey Bay. Suddenly he pointed and cried out, "A sign! A sign! *Gracias a Dios!* The *San Carlos* arrives with supplies from Mexico!"

The others crowded into the doorway. "A sign of what, Father?" De Anza asked, but he did not wait for an answer.

"I see what it is!" he exclaimed. "Come, *Señores,* let us sit at the table again. I will explain what I think the *Padre Presidente* means.

"This ship has come to unload the annual supplies for Monterey, is it not so? Now I appeal to your imaginations. After the *San Carlos* has unloaded this cargo, we place in her empty hold the provisions that have been warehoused here since last year for the San Francisco *presidio* and the two *pueblos.* Why not let the *San Carlos* also carry the vestments and other religious goods, together with tools and utensils for house and field, likewise warehoused here for the missions San Francisco de Asís and Santa Clara de Asís, which are destined to be erected near the harbor

of San Francisco, as all agree? The civilian and the
religious supplies can be kept separate in the ship's
holds, and if a bit of mixing should occur between
them, who cares?''

De Anza, well launched, went on planning aloud.
"I visualize, *Señores,* both a land party and a sea
party, with a rendezvous at San Francisco Bay. On
board the *San Carlos* go the women, the children,
and the ailing among my settlers. Lt. Moraga will
lead the land party, consisting of all the men. Among
them may ride, if you wish, *Padre Presidente,* four of
your priests, two each for the two contemplated missions. They will act as chaplains at first and later as
founders of the missions.

"Remember, *Señores,* that according to my agreement with Governor Rivera, no mission is to be
sited or erected until he arrives to approve the sites
and attend the dedications. But meantime the priests,
with the supplies for both missions, will be ready and
eager, but not so eager as to violate the agreement. A
command to your priests to that effect might well
come from you, *Padre Presidente.*''

"It will come," said Fr. Serra. "I will designate
Fr. Palóu and Fr. Cambón for Mission San Francisco
de Asís and, for Mission Santa Clara de Asís, Fr.
Murguia and Fr. Tomas de la Peña.''

The *Padre Presidente,* however, looked troubled.
He said gloomily, "My conscience has begun to accuse
me, *Señores,* because of the secrecy of these arrangements, unknown to our lawful Governor. Had I not
often, over the years, tried in vain to get our holy
St. Francis a mission on his bay, I could not join
you in this. Now, because our saint has been wronged,
to repair that injury I help to wrong the Governor. It
seems that on rare occasions God wants His will to
be done on this earth with a quietness—not a mis-

representation, but a quietness.

"But is this God's will or mine? I do not know. So I impose upon myself the penance of letting others found the saint's mission while my way leads by ship to Mission San Diego, which needs me."

Outside, Fr. Serra remounted his burro and, after blessing all present, rode away among the pines.

De Anza shook his great head like a man emerging from the sea.

"If I am to meet Governor Rivera as far as possible down El Camino Real, there must first be conferences, many and brief, with Moraga, with the leaders among the settlers, and with the four priests designated to go with them. Also with the captain and crew of the *San Carlos* and the keeper of the King's warehouses. You will serve me as secretary, Ixtil. After that, I ask you to ride south with me to help reach an accommodation with that unhappy Rivera. In that, too, you can serve me well as a go-between, if you are willing, until we reach your Mission San Luis Obispo. Do I ask too much, *amigo?*"

"Much, but not too much, Captain," Ixtil said with a smile. "You are a teacher. To serve you is always to learn more and more."

With the help of Lt. Moraga, Ixtil, and the priests, De Anza organized the land expedition and its supplies and obtained from Captain Vega of the *San Carlos* all the necessary agreements about cargo, passengers, and destination. On the morning of De Anza's departure southward along El Camino, with Ixtil and a dozen troopers, the sailors and the settlers stowed the last of the north-bound supplies abroad the *San Carlos.*

De Anza and his band encountered Governor Rivera and his escort south of Mission San Antonio, at the point where El Camino climbs to cross the low hills.

Dusk coming on, the Governor had encamped there for the night.

"Here we camp too," De Anza told his men, "just across the road from the Governor in this clump of *piñones*. Off with the saddles! Shelter close together, as usual. Ixtil and I go to confer amicably with his Excellency."

Outside Rivera's tent, the guard refused them entrance. "The Governor eats, *compadres*. He does not wish to talk to you yet."

"When, then?" inquired De Anza, making an effort at patience.

"Perhaps after his meal. Perhaps only in the morning. He will inform you later."

"Sangre de Dios!" De Anza exploded. "Tell him that I, De Anza, must speak with him on the King's business."

The guard slouched into the tent and did not slouch out again for ten minutes, *"Mañana,"* he reported.

De Anza pushed past the guard into the tent, Ixtil reluctantly following. Inside, the Governor looked up coldly from his food.

"Must you break in upon me even while I eat, De Anza?"

"No, I will stand here until the last crumb has been swallowed. Then we will talk."

"Please yourself, *Señor*."

The Governor shrugged and continued eating at the same slow pace. To Ixtil the man looked tired and tense, for all his elaborate mask of calm. Suddenly Rivera pushed his plate aside.

"I find myself not very hungry. Say what you have to say."

De Anza seized a box, pushed it to the table and sat down solidly upon it.

"What I have to say is this. Before leaving Monterey

for the peninsula, I wrote to your Excellency, outlining what I intended to perform there, as commissioned by the Viceroy, to wit: to select sites for a *presidio* and two *pueblos.* You did not do me the courtesy of writing to me in your turn. But let that pass. I now report, Excellency, that I selected those three sites, good ones, and showed them to my second in command, Lt. Moraga, who will now build the necessary structures to start a *presidio* and the *pueblos.*"

"You have omitted something, *Señor.* It is common knowledge in Monterey that you also selected sites for two missions, one at Dolores, the other on the Rio de Guadalupe. I am so informed."

"Then you have been misinformed, *Señor,*" De Anza declared with heat. "It is true that as we traveled up and down the peninsula, Fr. Font and I took note of several apt localities for the planting of missions, but we never once marked any of them for a mission or fixed upon any precise site. All that we intended was to point out the numerous possibilities on every hand in that general area. In that way we hoped to give Fr. Serra and his priests a preview of the alternatives open to them."

The Governor smiled triumphantly. "My information is that your inspection of some places was so minute as to constitute the choice of sites. That usurps my function as Governor."

"So now we come to definitions," De Anza growled. "Inspection is not selection. Fr. Font did not bless soil and water at any spot, did not set up any cross, did not build any altar or celebrate any Mass—all these actions being necessary preliminaries to the sacralization of a place chosen for the siting of a mission. He is here in my train. Ask him, if you wish to hear the truth of fact as against the misinformation of rumor."

Governor Rivera nodded. "I will hear him in the morning, after breakfast, Good night, *Señores.*" He rose and walked away.

"We are very curtly dismissed by this peasant from Asturias," De Anza commented bitterly to Ixtil as they returned to their camp.

"I have a thought," said Ixtil.

"Out with it, then."

"This Governor is as angry as you, *Commandante,* but controls his passions better. That gives him the advantage. Indeed, he skillfully insults you for purposes of his own."

"We are like oil and water, that man and I. We do not mix at all. Nevertheless you are right, Ixtil. I must rule my anger."

Before Fr. Font went to be questioned by Governor Rivera the next morning, De Anza gave him instructions.

"Show him freely your map of the peninsula. Encourage him to ask more and more questions about the location of the *presidio* and the proposed sites for the two *pueblos.* Without lying, pile detail upon detail— in the ways you scholars know so well. At some point he is sure to ask whether we selected mission sites. Use the same methods there to prolong discussion. Speculate on my intentions, on Lt. Moraga's point of view, on your own ideas, even on Ixtil's.

"We must move south, drawing him with us, to gain time for Moraga and the *San Carlos* to leave Monterey far behind, before the Governor arrives to forbid them. Let the ultimate answers to the questions he will direct to you seem to lie always on the other side of the next hill. You understand me, Father?"

Fr. Font smiled a rare smile. "I will do my best, *Señor.*"

His best was so good that when De Anza broke camp at midmorning, Rivera did likewise, and the two parties rode southward together, the Governor deep in conversation with Fr. Font, with De Anza, even with Ixtil.

What tricksters we men are by nature, Ixtil reflected. Here we are, playing a game in which the Governor loses, mile by mile, as we move from Monterey—and San Francisco. He will be justly furious when he learns. True, it is in the best of causes, and if Fr. Serra can keep his reservations about deceit, cannot I?''

Rivera did not detect the game that was being used to detain him until the joint cavalcade was descending Cuesta Pass, a few miles short of Mission San Luis Obispo. There, Ixtil reflected, he would be home at last, under no obligation to De Anza to continue the sad comedy.

The Governor's anger when he divined what was happening was anything but restrained: He rode furiously alongside De Anza's party, cursing them aloud.

"Whatever you have kept hidden from me in Monterey I shall prohibit!" he shouted. "And since you have drawn me so far south, I shall continue with you until you leave California, warning all men of your perfidy!''

He kept his word. He camped well outside the stockade of Mission San Luis, while De Anza greeted old friends inside, but once encamped, Rivera rode his horse into the coutyard to shout his accusations against De Anza. This tactic, borne stoically by De Anza, scandalized the priests of the mission and astonished their converts. Embarrassed, they stood about, watching this extraordinary quarrel of a Spanish Governor with one of his own race.

Fr. Mugártegui tried to turn all to laughter. "True,''

he remarked in a penetrating whisper which all could hear, "Fages was a better Governor than this one, and we should be glad to have him back. We should have remembered the refrain of the old woman in the story. 'God deliver us from a worse one!' "

He laughed at his joke, and everyone who heard it laughed too, except Fr. Joseph and Ixtil, who saw the tide of red suffuse Rivera's face, and pitied him. Shortly, the Governor returned to his camp outside.

"That man is half-crazed with friendlessness, and a sentence of excommunication not yet lifted," Ixtil confided to the priest. "I cannot bear to see him destroy himself like this. All the more because I have shared in the plan to decoy him away from Monterey until Lt. Moraga and others have time to set up on the peninsula of San Francisco Bay a *presidio* and two *pueblos,* as ordered by the Viceroy.

"I strongly suspect that Fr. Palóu and Fr. Cambon may have yielded to the temptation to at least start founding Mission San Francisco de Asís on La Laguna de Nuestra Señora de los Dolores, although Captain De Anza warned them not to. In that case, the Governor's anger is at least half justified, seeing that he has the prerogative to be present at the selection of sites and at the founding of any establishment on the sites."

Fr. Joseph listened incredulously. "You, Ixtil, helped to lure him away from his duties? Tell me the full story."

When Ixtil had recounted the events, Fr. Joseph sank into deep thought.

"It seems to me that all have erred. De Anza and Fr. Font must be persuaded to tell the whole truth to Rivera and to show him how to assert those remnants of his rights as Governor which still remain. And you, Ixtil, must take your part in this to the confessional."

Summoned by the priest, De Anza and Fr. Font came to stand before him. The two agreed without cavil, far more quickly than Ixtil expected, to do what Fr. Joseph solemnly advised. Ixtil thought to himself that he was always underestimating De Anza.

"I too have a conscience, Father," the latter admitted, "though sometimes it sleeps. But is has been wide awake lately, and especially today. I feel thoroughly ashamed. I will go personally to Governor Rivera and confess all, but not abjectly. Give me an hour or two in which to consider how best he may reestablish himself."

After several hours, which De Anza spent in the church, he emerged looking determined.

"Now comes a still harder part. Ixtil, Fr. Font, we ride to the Governor's camp. We answer with complete candor any and all questions which he may put to us about the peninsula. We consider his needs. No reticences, no elisions, no misleading, no lies."

Their welcome in the camp outside the mission was frostier than ever, from soldier-guards to Governor. Using all his charm, De Anza succeeded in getting admission to the Governor's presence for himself and his companions. He refused to notice Rivera's icy glare.

"You see us here as petitioners, *Señor Gubernador.* We have done you wrong. Fr. Joseph, that good priest, has taught us how to confess to you."

Surprise kept Rivera silent and the plain good will of his visitors opened his ears to listen. With confirming words from Ixtil and Fr. Font to back up his story at critical points, De Anza told the whole truth.

"Who am I to refuse forgiveness," Rivera said at its conclusion, "when I stand in need of it myself? I excuse you, and all the others who have acted against me in this episode. For breaking the law of sanctuary in San Diego, the priests there have ex-communicated me, cut me off from the Holy Eucharist, and left me alone in my loneliness. Fr. Font, is there no remedy?"

"Jesus died in order that every sin should have a remedy. God loves a humble and repentant heart, *Señor*. Go to the priests who cut you off, those in San Diego. Confess your error openly. By canon law, they are then bound to revoke their ban and to re-admit you to the sacraments."

"I must return to San Diego, then?"

"Yes, you must, But remember, to your comfort, that a long journey to the confessional is a short journey to heaven."

"Excellency," said De Anza, "Fr. Font has been prescribing measures for the healing of the spirit. May I advise you now of means to use in restoring your political position—a lesser matter, no doubt, but vital in its sphere?"

"I am listening, *Señor*. What you and your friends have done you can undo, perhaps."

"Not altogether undo, Excellency, for the past yields to no man. But I can at least suggest ways in which you may reinstate yourself into events at the point where they now stand, and govern them as they develop in the future."

"Looking backward, *Señor*," said Rivera, "I can see that you have a highly developed sense for politics. You should be a politician, not an explorer."

De Anza laughed. "I am both, Excellency. In this New World, God help any explorer who is not also a politician, though the reverse does not hold true. But to come down to facts. Though lacking recent news from Lt. Moraga, I am sure that by now he has started both a *presidio* and a *pueblo* at the penin-sula's tip. And my guess is that he has allowed Fr.

Palóu and Fr. Cambon to establish at least a provisional mission, probably on the lagoon named *Nuestra Senora de los Dolores,* only a few miles away. Beyond this, he cannot have had time to go.

"Write him an official letter, ordering him to build the *presidio* and a surrounding *pueblo* on the site designated by De Anza. Approve, also, the establishing of a mission, San Francisco de Asís, on the lagoon named for Our Lady of Sorrows, unless the priests there wish to choose some other spot not more than three miles distant. Furthermore, recommend that Moraga continue to search for a second *pueblo* site on the south bank of the *Rio de Nuestra Señora de Guadalupe,* there to construct a town suitable to those settlers of ours who did not wish to inhabit the tip of the peninsula.

"Finally, forbid him to consider any site or lay any stone for Mission Santa Clara. It is not for him but for you, as Governor acting in concert with Fr. Tomás de la Peña, to bring that mission into being."

"This Fr. Tomás—he has been appointed by Fr. Serra for the purpose?" A slight smile played about the lips of the Governor as he spoke.

"Yes," said De Anza, "Fr. Serra told me so in Monterey. Now one final step, necessary to re-establish your authority. You will be writing, as soon as possible, the foregoing letters to Moraga along the lines just described. I, too, will write him, when I reach Mission San Gabriel, to put himself under your command."

Rivera stretched, got up from his chair, and strode about the tent.

"Instead of going south to San Diego, I should be going north to the San Francisco peninsula. I am turned in the wrong direction."

"No, Excellency," De Anza insisted. "Removal of

the excommunication comes first. Without it, men will avoid you, and not hear your ordinances. Once freed from that burden, you can fly north like a swan whose whiteness will attract men's eyes—and their affections.''

Governor Rivera studied him with approval. *''Por Dios, Señor,* the skill with which you unwind so intricate a web is a marvel. To weave the web is difficult enough, but to unravel it without tearing takes the greater art.

''Let us then proceed together, amicably, to Mission San Gabriel, where we must part, you for the desert, I for San Diego. In confidence, *Señor,* what has hurt me most in this excommunication is not the separation from the sacraments, for I am a very bad Catholic, I fear, but the fact that it was pronounced by Fr. Lasuén, whom I love, and would have had as my personal chaplain, had not Fr. Serra denied it because of the scarcity of priests.''

De Anza nodded in sympathy. ''Then Fr. Lasuén's withdrawal of the ban will feel all the better, won't it?''

''It will indeed. So, southward ho!''

They rode away next morning, the two leaders side by side and their respective escorts mingled.

Chapter 12

Watching them go, Ixtil breathed a deep sign of relief. He did not enjoy intrigue in high places. His participation in it left him feeling soiled, his innocence, such as it was, stained with guilt which he could not endure. He sought relief through Fr. Joseph in the confessional. Because the penance was only to attend Mass every morning for a month, he sensed that it was too light and resolved to double the period to two months.

After Ysaga had finished her morning work of helping at the *monjerio,* the baby in his cradle on her back, he told her about everything. She held his hand while they walked back to their hut for the noonday meal.

"Ixtil is always Ixtil, and I shall love him always," she assured him, turning her dark eyes full upon him, "but I do not think you should mix so much in the matters of great men. They take you away from home, in distance and in what you think about. Come back to me and the baby. We have never decided on his Chumash name, you know."

Laughing, they tried out various names but none seemed to suit, until they hit upon Tilic. Ixtil liked it because it was short, Ysaga because it sounded a little like Ixtil. The baby did not seem to care what he was called. He was too busy, every moment he was awake, learning, with wondering eyes, about the world around him, and especially about the new, large being who made sounds at him and returned his smiles. This being differed from the other one, who had always been with him, in having a harder body and, alas, no source of food.

"This lad and I must get to know each other," said Ixtil, picking him up in his arms.

"Good," Ysaga agreed. "One of the best ways to get acquainted is for you to clean him with moss when he dirties himself, and to see that the moss where he sits in the cradle is always fresh."

"That is one for you, wife." Ixtil laughed. "You haven't changed, thank God. But it also follows that I should have my turn to carry him in his cradle wherever I go, so long as you are close by to feed him upon demand."

When he told her about his Mass penance, Ysaga smiled a little.

"Tilic and I will attend all the Masses with you. I don't think Tilic can have committed many sins yet, but he will learn about the Mass and the special prayers by hearing and watching in the church. And I must go with the two of you to nurse him if he cries. Even if we are not *Jesu, Maria y Jose,* we shall be a holy family."

They both laughed, and the child crowed. That was another happy day.

Fr. Joseph set Ixtil to conducting the adult catechism classes in the afternoons. The fact that one of their own race, though only a young man, could speak and write in both Chumash and Spanish drew many of the parents whose children had been baptized by the priests. Having been drawn to the class by curiosity and racial pride, they became interested in what was being taught, and numbers of them in due course accepted the *doctrina católica*. Whenever Ixtil found a man or woman who he thought was ripe for conversion, they would talk together for hours or days, sitting on the earth in the sun in the mission garden or on the porch of the priests' house when the sun was too hot.

In this way Ixtil came to know in confidence the troubles of his people having to do with faith. And there were few, he thought, which did not yield in one degree or another to prayer. So Ixtil taught his pupils how to pray to Jesus, Who, as the Good Shepherd, always moved among them and loved them. Ixtil composed petitions of thanksgiving, reconcilation, repentance, and reparation for all their sins and for the sins of others. He gave them strings of glass beads, properly spaced so as to constitute rosaries, and taught what prayers to say, and with what thought, for each decade. Also, he often described each step in the Mass and its meaning. He had them memorize the Our Father particularly, in both the Spanish and the Chumash tongues. They especially delighted to say his Chumash version beginning: *"Dios cascoco upalequen Alaipai quia—enicho opte; paquinini juch quique etchuet cataug itimi tiup caneche Alaipai. . ."* *

When Ixtil had taught them as much as he knew, he sent his best students to Fr. Joseph for correction and polishing. Some, he thought in despair, would never reach that advanced stage because of his own failure to stimulate them to learn the faith. He was convinced that very few of them were really stupid. For reasons beyond his knowledge, they lacked any interest in language.

It occurred to him one day that such students could more easily attain the faith through their hands and eyes than through their ears, through listening to

---

*From Fr. Maynard Geiger O.F.M., *Indians of Mission Santa Barbara*, p. 24.

sounds and repeating them with the tongue, without the sense having penetrated the brain. Accordingly, on one occasion, striving to reach one of the backward ones, he carved idly with his knife at a piece of soft wood, as if unaware of what he was doing. Under his cutting and smoothing, the figure of a man took shape. The backward one stopped trying to listen to Ixtil's words and gazed, all eyes, at the shape emerging from the wood, soon easily recognizable as Jesus praying, perhaps in the garden at Gethsemane. Ixtil took good care to give Him a Chumash face. In Palestine He might have a Jewish face, in Mexico the face of an Aztec, but in Tixlini He must look like a Chumash in order to draw the tribes to Him.

"Like to try it?" Ixtil asked, offering his knife.

"Oh, yes!" the man said.

Ixtil had several chunks of soft wood, and soon the man who felt terrified by words was proving that he felt no terror at all for wood. After some initial fumbling, the knife in his hands came alive, as if it knew exactly where to cut, where to smooth, in order to call out ultimate sadness in the expression of Jesus.

Ixtil laid in a supply of soft wood and of knives large and small, but all very sharp. Before he knew it, all those who were backward with words had begun to carve the holy figures of the Bible. No genius towered among the carvers, but several of them grew to be extremely skilled in both design and wood carving. And the more skilled, the more pious they became.

What we do makes us what we are, Ixtil reflected. Each holy statue carved is a prayer.

Fr. Joseph dropped by one day to watch. "Superb, Ixtil!" he exclaimed when the class ended. "I do not mean the statues, through many of them are good. I mean the piety bred and fed by the sculpture. You have devised a method of teaching the faith—none better—to the convert who worships best by the art of his hands. May I suggest painting also?''

Ixtil nodded, smiling. "That is another art, certainly.''

Lucky for him, he thought, that he had worked on the rock paintings under the eye of Werowance. And that he had seen Fr. Font's picture of Our Lady of Guadalupe. He could tell his small class what some of them already knew: the many shades of color in manifold earths and rocks, in streams and cliff faces, in the flowers and berries of the meadow, in the flotsam washed up on the beaches by the tides, as well as how to mix and apply them. It was Ysaga who thought of painting on the inside of leftover pieces of well-scraped sheephide, dried and softened.

When Fr. Joseph came again, the priest asked hesitantly, "Do you think that the painters might become so absorbed in their art as to forget its purpose, which is to know God?''

"That can happen, Father,'' Ixtil admitted, "but I try to prevent it by allowing only holy art. They may paint or carve nothing except the saints and people or scenes from the Scriptures. That gives them material ample enough to last until doomsday. Often, while they work, I read aloud some passage or other from Holy Writ.''

Fr. Joseph surveyed with care each product of Ixtil's *bodega,* as he called it in fun. "Tell your students,'' he said, "that a week from today I will select one painting and one carving for display in the church. We need especially the Madonna and portrayals of Jesus at different times of His life. We could use one of St. Francis, too, with the stigmata. God bless the work!''

After this promise the *bodega* flourished as never before. The best of those works which the church did not select began appearing in the dwellings of the converts around the mission, acting as great aids to knowledge and prayer.

In the second moon of the year belonging to Our Lord, 1777, a calvalcade rode past the mission, going to Monterey, but it did not stop. The word went round that its leader was no other than *Señor* Neve, the new Governor. This was Ixtil's first inkling that Governor Rivera had been replaced by the Viceroy. The quick glimpse he had of the new Governor revealed a face cold and secretive, and unspeakably self-possessed. Ixtil feared him and what he might do, but then he remembered how he had first hated Rivera, too. He decided to reserve judgment.

Some days later, Rivera and his escort came riding south and stopped overnight at the mission. Rivera, freed from the strains of responsibility, was a new man. He had reverted to what he was by nature, a blunt and comradely soldier who had confidence in his abilities, and showed it. He was almost happy, almost gay.

"*Hola,* Ixtil!" he shouted on seeing him. "You are seeing now the real Rivera, what I was meant to be. No more intrigues, no more pretenses, no more hesitations between this and that. They thought they were demoting me. Instead they have set me free. Congratulate me, Ixtil!"

"*Señor,* I do, with all my heart."

"De Anza did not speak against me to the Viceroy. Never think it! That excommunication fracas at Mission San Diego did the business. I thank those priests every night in my prayers." He smiled to himself. "They thought they were cutting me off from *el Dios bueno.* Instead, they have joined me closer to Him."

Ixtil did not want Rivera to think of the San Diego priests as his enemies. "I am sure," he told Rivera, "that they wished, those priests, exactly that outcome for you from the first. They are not vengeful men but teachers."

Rivera turned grave. "Perhaps. You are too idealistic about priests, Ixtil. They are not all angels with wings. But about Fr. Lasuén and his mates I am willing to believe the best. It is my weakness to forgive too slowly."

At that point Fr. Joseph carried Rivera off to dinner with the other clergy. Later, he told Ixtil that Captain Rivera was on his way back to Mexico City to receive a purely military assignment. Ixtil was to hear no more of him until his death by massacre among the Yumas several years later.

In the time of falling leaves in the year belonging to God, 1778, a courier galloped in with the news that Fr. Serra was coming to the mission to administer the sacrament of confirmation. Fr. Cavaller and Fr. Paterna went into hurried action.

"This is a very notable spiritual opportunity, Ixtil," Fr. Joseph told him. "So far, we have never been able to administer this sacrament to those we have baptized because California has not had a bishop. But now Fr. Serra has received from our Holy Father the Pope special powers to confer it. Fr. Paterna and I want every one of our converts to receive this gift of the Holy Spirit. Those who reside at the mission or just outside it can be summoned easily. But there are many in the baptismal record whose names I have forgotten—God pardon me—in the outlying villages. They must be told to come quickly, while Fr. Serra is here. We expect him the day after tomorrow. He will probably stay no more than a week since he still has the four northern missions to visit. We give you, Ixtil, that work—to ride out and bring in the far-off ones."

"We have about nine days from now, then?" Ixtil asked.

"At most. Better aim at a week," Fr. Joseph said. "We've worked out a day-by-day itinerary for you."

Ixtil studied the plan. "This should work well," he said at last, "provided you have men with spare horses and *caretas* to meet me wherever I'm to be each evening. These will be for the converts who are too young or too old, lame, or sick to walk on their own two legs. Most can walk, but always there are some who cannot."

"Start with the most distant villages," the priest suggested, "and work inward."

"Yes, that makes sense," Ixtil agreed. "I hope we'll have enough horses and *caretas* for those who need them."

Fr. Cavaller looked thoughtful. "I pray we have. We'll mobilize our full resources in transportation, and leave the outcome to God."

Ixtil spent the ensuing week riding from village to village, telling all the Christians about the strong new sacrament which would help to save them by the power of the Holy Spirit.

After carrying the weak ones to the places of transportation, the walkers usually started for the mission in a body, though generally a few stragglers turned up late. As the end of the week approached, Ixtil and the horse he rode were helping directly in the movement of people, as the hopelessly delayed had to be given a lift on the way. After the great in-gathering, with all its special needs, had been completed, Ixtil calculated that few converts—if any—had failed to get to the mission in time, by one means or another.

When, at week's end, he rode wearily into the

mission compound, he found to his great pleasure that Fr. Serra was still there. Moreover, he learned, the *Padre Presidente* had delayed his departure in order to administer the sacrament to him. At first he felt abashed, but all such feeling evaporated when the intense little priest swept Ixtil into his arms, exclaiming, "Welcome! Welcome! It is always Ixtil who is given the longest, hardest role to play, and always he plays it well. God will repay you, my son, far better than my poor thanks ever can."

Ixtil's heart went out to the *Padre,* who had cared enough to wait for him. "Nevertheless, Father, here on earth it is always your words I hear, giving me thanks for few and little deeds. You make me feel useful."

At the Mass that evening, Ixtil received confirmation in the presence of all. Afterward, he and Ysaga were invited to eat at the table of the priests, and during the meal the talk was grave. Fr. Serra read a letter from his deputy in Monterey warning that Governor Neve had said on several public occasions that Fr. Serra was not a bishop and that his *patente* for administering confirmation, though issued by the Holy Father himself from Rome, was void in California because it had not been approved by the *pase* of Spain's King Carlos.

A long silence ensued; then Fr. Paterna spoke indignantly.

"I don't understand, *Padre Presidente.* What in the world has a Governor of California—be he a Neve, a Rivera, a Fages, or anyone else—to say about a *patente* granted by the Holy Father in Rome bestowing on you the necessary faculties?"

Fr. Serra smiled faintly. "Nothing in the world, Antonio, once the King has endorsed it with his *pase.* But this is exactly what our Governor Neve denies—that the document bears the King's *pase.*"

Fr. Joseph looked startled for a moment; then he spoke.

"Ah yes. I must be growing senile. I had forgotten, fool that I am! Our Spanish kings have retained to themselves the power to veto any appointment made by the Pope in their New World territories. In effect, the *patente* to Fr. Serra from Rome appoints him temporarily a kind of bishop, since only bishops may give the sacrament of confirmation. So the question is whether King Carlos has approved the Pope's appointment by affixing the royal *pase.* Am I correct, *Padre Presidente?*"

"Exactly correct, Joseph," said Fr. Serra.

"But surely your *patente* bears the *pase?*"

"So I believe, but I cannot prove it at a moment's notice. The original document is kept, of course, in the archives of our Mother House of San Fernando in Mexico City. I have not seen it, but neither has Neve. I've written him, expressing the conviction that my superiors would never have sent me a summary of the *patente* unless it bore the King's *pase.* He rejects that argument and demands sworn statements by the Viceroy, as well as by my superiors, that the King's *pase* is indeed affixed."

"How long will all that take?" Fr. Paterna asked.

"What with one thing and another, at least a year or two," replied Fr. Serra sadly. "You see, the situation is complicated by the fact that our good friend Bucareli has just lost his authority as Viceroy over a large group of provinces along Mexico's northern border. These include California. The King's Council for the Indies has reorganized them, for their better defense, as *Las Provincias Internas,* and has given command over them to a military man, Teodoro de Croix, who cares little for missions. He and Neve are of the same stamp, I think."

Another long silence fell over the dinner table. Finally, Fr. Joseph broke it throughtfully.

"To amplify what the *Padre Presidente* has just said about Neve's view of our missions, I have heard from several sources that the Governor does not think of us at all in the Franciscan way but as *doctrinas,* or parishes, of some Mexican bishop."

"*Nombre de Dios,* which bishop?" asked Fr. Paterna.

Fr. Joseph shrugged his shoulders. "Reports from Monterey are that he is careful not to commit himself. Sometimes he says the Bishop of Durango, sometimes the Bishop of Guadalajara, sometimes another. It really makes no difference. Observe his strategy. If we belong in the diocese of any bishop, no matter which, only that bishop can give confirmation in our missions. So both the *patente* and the *pase* are by-passed. Also, we are cut off from the superiors of our order in Mexico City and attached instead to the bishop. In effect, we become his parish priests, whom he can transfer here and there as he pleases. We become subject, also, to all his edicts in the running of every mission."

Fr. Serra listened to Fr. Cavaller carefully, his brows creased with a frown. "A notable exposition, Joseph," he applauded grimly at the end. "I agree completely. This Neve begins to look like a devious and complex man, far more dangerous to us and to the Franciscan mission system than he seems to be on the surface. The question is, what's to be done? I seek advice from each of you, though I do not promise to follow it. Ixtil?"

Ixtil felt himself in very deep waters, but he saw one thing clearly.

"Nothing should stop the *Padre Presidente* from giving the confirmation sacrament. That is a thing of religion. It cannot give way to the whims of governors, who deal only with secular things."

Ysaga smiled at him, nodding, as Ixtil added, "My wife, Ysaga, thinks the same, *Señores.*"

Fr. Serra looked pleased. "Father Paterna?"

"Go on with the confirming, whether Neve likes it or not. He cannot put you in that Monterey jail of his without creating a scandal which would tear California apart. How else can he stop you?"

"Direct confrontation, eh?" remarked Serra. "Father Cavaller?"

"First, of course, write to the Viceroy and to our College of San Fernando, requesting examination of your *patente* and verification that it bears the King's *pase.* But for the sake of our baptized ones, you should not delay the giving of confirmation for years while you wait for the verification to arrive. Continue administering the rite, but with little noise. In my opinion, Neve will look the other way, for fear of too great a blow to his authority when the *pase* is found in good order, as he well knows it will be."

"And what about his claim that our missions are only *doctrinas,* parishes that teach under some bishop?"

"A dangerous gambit, Father, as he must be aware— so dangerous that I cannot conceive why he risks it." Fr. Joseph, shaking his head, paused in puzzlement. "Even his military superior, De Croix, may not like to have bishops, instead of Franciscan missionaries, running all over his provinces. Leave the next move to Neve. Let us see how he extricates himself.

"Meantime, write letters to the Viceroy, to our college, even to De Croix himself. Also to every friend you have, from Mexico to Madrid, describing the difficulties you foresee. A petition signed by all the California missionaries could be useful, too."

Fr. Serra's face still wore a worried frown. "Thank you, all of you, *compadres,* for sharing your wisdom with me. Now I must weigh duties. So many duties! To our *Indios,* whom we guide toward salvation; to our Franciscan brothers, here and in Ciudad de Mexico; to the secular authorities, to whom, St. Paul warns us, we are subject; and to Mother Church, God's instrument. If only I were a simple priest, not a *presidente* of anything which raises so many problems, and so tangled!"

He rose from his chair, "*Señores,* your forgiveness, please, and your prayers. I must leave for Mission San Antonio within the hour."

Chapter 13

In the weeks that followed, the news drifting down El Camino to San Luis Obispo told that, at Mission San Antonio, Fr. Serra confirmed many hundreds of converts, collected there for him by its busy priests. At his home mission, San Carlos, he confirmed hundreds more, who came in from their *rancherias* to welcome him. He made no effort, however, to bring in those who did not come. And when Governor Neve cited the lack of a *pase* as a pretext for refusing the *Presidente* the usual military escort on a journey to confirm the neophytes at Mission Santa Clara and Mission San Francisco de Asís, Fr. Serra registered an official protest but did not insist on going alone. Instead, he remained quietly at San Carlos.

Three weeks later, a long procession of *Indios* from those two missions, led by their priests, walked through Monterey to Mission San Carlos, requesting aloud to be confirmed, while from his balcony Governor Neve looked on, powerless.

Fr. Serra gladly complied. And from that time on it became a custom for priests from the nearby northern missions to bring their converts to Mission San Carlos for confirmation whenever they had a sufficient number to justify the journey.

At last, in the time of budding leaves in the year belonging to God, 1782, the *Padre Presidente* sent an open letter by courier to the priests of all his missions. At San Luis Obispo, Fr. Cavaller read it aloud to the other clergy, to Ixtil, and to Cpl. Briones:

> Finally, brothers, nearly three years after our Governor Neve expressed his first doubt that the King's *pase* had been affixed to my *patente* from the Holy Father to perform the rite of Confirmation, his doubts and those of all others of like mind have been happily resolved. The lost *pase* has been found or, better, it has never truly been lost. Inspectors representing the Viceroy, together with other inspectors representing our College of San Fernando, have seen it with their own eyes, affixed to my *patente,* and all have so certified under oath. This certification has been sent to both Governor Neve and to his superior, Commander Theodoro de Croix. Letters from these two last-named officials have reached me, authorizing me to proceed with such Confirmations as may be necessary to the Catholic Faith. Praise be to Jesus, Mary, and Joseph!
>
> I shall soon be visiting each Mission again in order to confer the sacrament on those who have become eligible since my former visit.
>
> > Junipero Serra, O.F.M.
> > *Presidente*

"So it ends," Fr. Joseph commented thankfully as he refolded the letter. "I still wonder what Neve thought he could gain by his frivolous fiction."

As Ixtil went off to his newest work in the carpenter shop, Fr. Paterna swore a most unpriestly oath. "What he has gained is to hamper the missions, which—out of sheer malice—he detests. Not a single new mission has been founded for four years. And God alone knows how many thousands of gentiles have perished meantime, either without learning the Christian faith at all or without being confirmed in it by the sacrament of the Holy Spirit. There's gain for you! The man has been doing the work of the Devil, whom he resembles."

Fr. Joseph retained his accustomed mildness. "That may be, Antonio, but he has not hurt us as much as all that, at least not in the number of confirmations. Probably we in the five northern missions have managed, in one way or another, to confirm very nearly as many of the recently baptized as we would have under normal circumstances. The lack of new missions—well, that is a more serious matter."

A small enclosure in the letter spun to the floor. Picking it up, Fr. Joseph saw writing on it, which he read aloud: " 'A private note addressed especially to Mission San Luis Obispo by Fr. Serra.' Let's see . . . He informs us that arrangements are taking shape for the founding of three new missions and a *presidio* along the channel, the missions to be named for San Buenaventura, Santa Barbara, and Purísima Concepción. Antonio, we may have to take back some of the ugly things we've been saying about Neve and his failure to authorize new missions."

"I'll unsay them when I see these proposed missions actually in existence," Fr. Paterna said curtly.

Fr. Joseph's eyes moved down the page of the private note.

"He says that vast quantities of supplies are being gathered at Mission San Gabriel. An astonishing number of people have arrived there, too, including women and children. Oh, I see. There has been another wholesale importation of married settlers under the former Governor Rivera, as in the second De Anza expedition—apparently hundreds. No definite destination is mentioned for them, but Fr. Serra thinks they have come to establish a big *pueblo* a few miles away from Mission San Gabriel. Far enough from that mission and the three others proposed, I hope, so as not to spoil them with the deadly proximity of a large *pueblo*.

"There is much to study in this special note addressed to us. Governor Neve is at San Gabriel too, where

it seems that all the world is gathering. Fr. Serra
himself will be passing through here, on his way to
San Gabriel, within a week. A *week!* He wants to
take Ixtil south with him, but gives no reasons. Fr.
Paterna, please send a message to Ixtil asking him to
come here, *pronto.* He must know about this."

On his arrival, Fr. Joseph showed him the letter
and Ixtil perused it slowly. "I suspect," Fr. Joseph
told him, "that the *Padre Presidente* wants you as
an interpreter, adviser, friend, and general factotum.
Can you go?"

Ixtil thought for a few moments before replying.

"Yes, I think so. In fact, I know so. Ysaga is
pleased with the health of our two boys and of
Chiquita, our baby girl. My work in the carpenter
shop can be done by any of the men there. How
long will this new enterprise consume, do you think,
Father?"

"It's hard to say. Not more than two or three
months, probably, depending on the problems which
arise. Fr. Serra attracts problems as flowers in bloom
attract bees, as you know."

Ixtil smiled and nodded. "One learns many things
from being with him. I am anxious to go. Will there
be more confirmations this time?"

Fr. Joseph returned his smile and nodded. "You
remind me that the *Padre Presidente* will undoubtedly
take the time to give the sacrament to the 148 gentiles
baptized since his visit in 1778. Will you see to it,
as before, that our new converts in outlying villages
arrive in time to receive the sacrament? You know what
to do."

"Yes, I remember, *Padre.* But do you remember all
the details on your side of the ingathering? The messengers on horseback, the mules, the *caretas,* the rendezvous centers, the timing—everything?"

Fr. Joseph assured Ixtil that he did.

The operation went smoothly from the first. In three days at Mission San Luis Obispo, Fr. Serra confirmed the 148 candidates. His unexpected campanion, Fr. Cambón, had no authority to confirm, but he proved to be a great help in spiritually preparing those who were about to receive the sacrament. Fr. Cambón was one of those irritatingly deliberate men who do everything slowly but with utmost thoroughness.

In three days the priests rode off southward, Ixtil with them, and reached Mission San Gabriel with a speed which would not have shamed even one of those tireless couriers who carried private letters and public proclamations from the capital at Monterey.

On arrival at San Gabriel, Fr. Serra's party found the mission buildings and grounds thickly overpopulated. Governor Neve and his aides took up several rooms. But the mission's priests, though themselves crowded, managed to find room for Fr. Serra and Fr. Cambón.

Seeing that there could be no space for him to sleep inside, Ixtil explored the grounds for a place where he could bed down. All the available space inside the stockade, however, was overrun by families newly arrived from Mexico. Children roamed everywhere, while their soldier-fathers lounged about, waiting for something to happen, and their mothers cooked over compfires, gossiping with one another as they cooked.

Ixtil fell into conversation with one of the soldiers, named Pablo, and learned that they had all been recruited in Mexico as settlers.

"We are here either to guard some new missions from the heathen or to begin a big new *pueblo* to be called Nuestra Señora La Reina de los Angeles. Personally, I would prefer the mission work. My wife is a holy woman, sometimes too holy—you understand?—

and wants to live near a mission church." Pablo
shrugged. "There will be more quietness in my family
if we do that. You understand?"

Ixtil understood. "But how did you get here? Who
commands?"

"I leave you to judge, *amigo.* It is a sad story.
Captain Rivera recruited us in Sonora—the Captain
who used to be Governor of California. We all assembled at Alamos in Sonora, where he divided us
into two more or less equal groups. One he gave
to Lt. José de Zuñiga to come up by land through
Baja. The other he kept for himself, wishing to cross
the desert of the Yumas as De Anza did. I happened
to be in the Captain's party.

"All went well until we reached the Yumas, those
treacherous dogs. The Captain sent most of his company ahead, including me, but himself stayed with a
few men to rest his pack mules, which he thought
carried too much. There, he and those with him
were murdered in their sleep. Not one escaped. "I
lost my friend Felipe there. But I, having been assigned to the party which was sent ahead, escaped
death." He gave his habitual shrug.

"And the others, those with Lt. Zuñiga?" Ixtil
asked.

"No attack, no losses. They are all here. So if you
ask who commands us now, my answer is probably
the Lieutenant—but perhaps also Neve. We shall see."

This news of the death of Rivera hurt Ixtil in his
conscience. "The poor Captain!" he exclaimed, hanging his head. "May *el Dios bueno,* who understands
everything, make perpetual light shine upon his soul."

"You knew him?" Pablo asked with curiosity.

"A little, Pablo. Too little."

"One feels about these things."

"Yes, one feels."

Excusing himself, Ixtil left to inspect the mission courtyard. Just inside the walls, household and farming equipment of every sort for the projected *pueblo,* Nuestra Senora La Reina de los Angeles, was stacked in orderly heaps. In a corral, the horses, mules and asses, which had brought them safely all the way from Mexico, stamped and milled about. They were well fed and restive. In another area, the mountains of goods destined for the three new missions and a presidio had been assembled. Fr. Serra was counting them with care.

"Out of such confusion can order ever come?" Ixtil asked him.

"Oh, *si,*" the *Padre Presidente* replied. "Governor Neve is concerning himself only with his beloved *pueblo,* which at least he has had the grace to name after Our Lady of the Angels, and with his *presidio,* where most of the soldiers will be garrisoned. We, on the other hand, concern ourselves only with the goods needed for founding the three missions."

Some forty-eight of the settlers enlisted by Rivera chose to live in the *pueblo* to be erected some six miles south from Mission San Gabriel. They were the first to move out, including many of the women and children. Lt. Zuñiga led the way. This separation between *pueblo* and mission pleased Governor Neve less than Fr. Serra.

The latter's long patience in waiting for the three missions that were about to come into existence had its reward at last when Neve ordered that everyone properly concerned with the founding of the three missions, and of the new *presidio* too, should be ready to travel on March 26 of the year belonging to God, 1782, the Tuesday of Holy Week. The Indian town renamed Asumpta, for the Assumption of the Blessed Virgin Mary into heaven, had been agreed upon by

the religious and military authorities as a fitting location for the mission to be given to San Buenaventura.

On the date set, the Governor left San Gabriel at
the head of a long column: Fr. Serra's little group,
followed by eighty soldiers and their families led by
Sgt. Ortega, then by some Christian Indians, some
muleteers, and a train of a thousand cattle and pack
animals, many of them loaded with church goods and
equipment for house and field.

"At last," sighed Fr. Serra as the gate of Mission
San Gabriel. closed behind the last of the procession.
But he spoke too soon. A tired messenger on an
almost foundered horse rode up to Governor Neve and
handed him a letter.

"I recognize that messenger," said Fr. Serra. "He
has been with Captain Fages from the beginning. What
is he doing here?"

After reading the letter, Neve held up his hand to
signal a general stop. "In this letter," he announced
loudly, "Captain Fages says he wants to consult me
personally about launching a punitive force against
the Yuma Indians who killed the former Governor
Rivera y Moncada and Fr. Jalme. I must return to
the mission briefly to speak with him when he arrives.
Sgt. Ortega will lead your column to Asumpta, as
agreed. Expect me back in a day or two."

When Neve had ridden off with his escort, Fr.
Serra's voice rang down the long line of people: "Let
us say a prayer for the soul of *Señor* Rivera, who
died doing his duty: one Pater Noster, followed by
five Ave Marias, please." All said the prayer with
great reverence.

Sgt. Ortega led his expedition into Asumpta in the
closing days of March. "Where would you like to locate
the Mission San Buenaventura, *Padre?*" he asked.

Fr. Serra rose in his stirrups to survey the landscape. "Not too close to Asumpta, certainly. Pitch your camp in that big meadow, Sergeant. I would like to take a closer look at the surroundings."

Fr. Serra searched for two days, until he found good farming land in a valley traversed by a goodly river, a mile or more back from the ocean. There, on March 31, in the year belonging to God, 1782, he raised and blessed the cross, sang high Mass at an altar inside a brushwood shelter, and preached. It was Easter morning.

Next day, everybody was helping to build a more permanent chapel, together with living quarters for Fr. Cambón and for the five soldiers of the guard. They also built stables, corrals, carpenter shops, and other requisites. The whole they surrounded with a strong stockade.

Eleven days after the founding, Governor Neve and his bodyguard quietly rode in among the activities. Still mounted, still silent, his thin lips pressed together, he watched all that was going on. Fr. Serra walked over to greet him and was met by a cold stare.

"I see you have stolen a march on me, Fr. Serra," said the Governor resentfully.

"What march, *Señor?*"

"The march of setting this mission up as an independent unit, self-supporting and self-contained, not as a parish church of the new *pueblo* of Our Lady Queen of Angels, as it ought to be."

"But the *pueblo* is several miles away, *Señor.*"

"Then you should have moved the mission nearer."

"No, *Señor,* we should not. We are missionaries. We came to California to convert *Indios* to our Catholic faith, not to celebrate Mass in a *pueblo* which is Christian already. This is the Franciscan way, as your Excellency well knows."

"If so, it is a stiff-necked way, and proud, and

singular. Will Fr. Cambón ride to the *pueblo* to teach the people?"

"No, *Señor*. He will be alone here, and too busy. We are short of priests, though half a dozen more are on their way. As soon as Mission San Buenaventura has three priests, instead of only one, it will be able to help out in the *pueblo* churches. Meantime, Mission San Gabriel, which is fully staffed, can better spare a priest than can this new mission, which is just being built. Ask them."

"Perhaps I shall." Then he shouted, "Sgt. Ortega! Prepare all your people to leave at first light tomorrow—for Santa Barbara."

"A malicious man, this Governor," Ixtil said to Fr. Serra.

"Malicious when crossed, like most of us," Fr. Serra said mildly. Ixtil saw that the priest wanted to change the subject.

"Who was San Buenaventura, *Padre?*" he ventured to ask.

"A saint it is always beneficial to think about. Many consider him the second founder of our order. After the death of St. Francis, we lacked agreement as to how we should go on. As the elected head of all Franciscans, San Buenaventura brought us to agreement in a common sense of purpose. A great theologian, too. But, for our order, most of all a clearheaded and tactful administrator. I invoke him often in my prayers when problems of administration baffle me. I don't know why God made an administrator of me, for truly I am none."

Ixtil smiled a little. "The priests who serve under you do not think so," he said.

Neve led the slightly diminished cortege of soldiers and settlers ten leagues to the northwest, to the place

Fr. Crespi had named *La Laguna de la Concepción,* probably because it was near the Point named for the Immaculate Conception. According to instructions sent from Mexico to Neve and to Fr. Serra, a *presidio* and a mission were to be founded at or near that place. As they approached it, Ixtil was surprised to see Neve and his staff galloping ahead. He pointed out their haste to Fr. Serra, who evidently had noticed it already.

"Why should the Governor want to get there first?" Ixtil asked.

"To preempt the best spot for his *presidio,* I suppose. Since a mission is to be set up here, in addition to a *presidio,* he does not wish us to get there first,"

The priest chuckled aloud. "He does not understand, it seems, that the requirements for a Franciscan mission are quite different from those for an army post. Let him have his choice first. We will not compete with him."

Fr. Serra's words were borne out as the rest of the train moved wearily into camp. The Governor had selected for his *presidio* a commanding height overlooking the sea. He and his aides galloped about, setting up markers to outline the boundaries of the fort.

As soon as he saw Fr. Serra, Neve beckoned to him and announced categorically: "The *presidio* will be begun here, and be completed, before anyone lays a finger to your mission."

Fr. Serra did not grow angry, as the Governor expected.

"For the sake of peace," he said calmly, "I make no objection to such a priority, provided it is understood that Mission Santa Barbara is to be built immediately after the *presidio* is finished."

"It will be built," said Neve curtly.

Ixtil did not like the way his answer was phrased, but since Fr. Serra seemed satisfied he said nothing.

On the morning of April 21, 1782, the Feast of the Patronage of St. Joseph, Fr. Serra blessed the soil of the *presidio,* erected and blessed a cross, offered a low Mass, and preached. At the end, everyone sang the "Alabado." Ixtil acted as altar boy.

After the ceremony, Fr. Serra prepared a baptismal register for the *presidio's* church, as he did for all the churches he established. Using Ixtil as his amanuensis, he dictated the entry to be inscribed. Calling the new foundation "this New Mission and Royal *Presidio* of Santa Barbara," he dedicated it to that saint, "Virgin and Martyr, on the land of Yamnolit. I was and am alone, and therefore the Holy Mass was a Low Mass, and in place of *Te Deum* we had the *Alabado,* which is the equivalent of the *Laudamus.* May God bless it. Amen."

Ixtil understood all of this except the part calling the new foundation "this New Mission and Royal *Presidio.*" He ventured to ask the *Padre Presidente* about it. "Is not a place either a mission or a *presidio?* How can it be both at the same time?"

"A good question, Ixtil; you are right, of course. We have had precedents at both San Diego and Monterey, which at first were both presidios and missions. The dual roles did not work. In both cases the mission had to be separated from the presidio and moved several miles away so that it might function truly as a mission to the *Indios.*"

"I see, Father. You are depending on the promise of Governor Neve to construct your mission when he has completed the *presidio?*"

"Yes, I am. He has given his word. You speak as if you distrusted him. Do you?"

"Yes, Father."

"At least you speak honestly. But *I* must trust him. He is the Governor of this territory and a *caballero* of Spain."

Three weeks dragged on after completion of the *presidio,* and Governor Neve gave no sign of intending to build anything more. After all that waiting, Fr. Serra took Ixtil with him to speak to the Governor, who received them coldly.

"I know your complaint. You are here to ask me, 'Why is not my mission being founded and built?'" For these words, attributed to Fr. Serra, Neve pitched his voice in the wheedling tone of a beggar.

"Well, the answer is that you shall have your mission when it is conceived as it ought to be—not as a farm to be run for the profit of lazy *Indios* but as a *doctrina* for my good Catholic soldiers and settlers, erected near or in the presidio and the pueblo which will grow within its protection. The mission helps the presidio. The presidio helps the mission."

"And the *Indios,* to whom we are sent as Christian missionaries by our house in San Fernando, as authorized by the government in Mexico City—your superiors, Governor—who helps the *Indios?*"

"They can live in their surrounding villages and come to the Masses you will offer on Sundays, if they don't mind walking a mile or two. Or you can send priests out to their villages to instruct them and to pray the Mass in their native dialects. That should be enough to satisfy your itch for self-sacrifice."

Fr. Serra restrained his anger. "I have told you many times, *Señor,* as have many others, that under such a system, or rather lack of system, it becomes impossible to convert, genuinely convert, the *Indios* to our faith. And equally impossible to teach them the skills they must have in trades and occupations useful to civil life."

"That is a Franciscan dream," sneered Neve. "Until you found missions as I and the Jesuits and the Augustinians, and all good bearers of the Word, conceive them, no new ones will be built in California." Neve smiled at them fixedly.

"Be it so, *Señor*. Come, Ixtil."

"What will you do now, Father?" Ixtil inquired as Fr. Serra limped back to their camp in the meadow where their three mules could graze on grass, already almost dry enough to be cut and stacked as hay.

"Leave—if you will be good enough to load our gear on the pack mule and saddle the two we ride on."

Ixtil gladly did so. This place had not been good for the *Padre Presidente*. He looked deeply sad and very old.

"North or south?" Ixtil asked.

"North, back to Mission San Carlos, my earthly home."

Chapter 14

They traveled El Camino very slowly, with frequent roadside stops by day and long camps overnight.

At Mission San Luis Obispo, after one look at his face, Fr. Joseph put the *Presidente* to bed.

Fr. Serra thanked him ruefully. "I bring you trouble again, Joseph. Always trouble. But do not pamper me too much."

"All you need is a rest, Father, and that is easy to give."

After the *comida* that evening, Ixtil told of the events at San Gabriel, the founding of Mission San Buenaventura, and the perfidy of Governor Neve at Santa Barbara.

"I wish I could give the *Presidente* a rest in bed for several weeks," said Fr. Joseph, "but already he is asking how many new candidates we have for confirmation, preliminary to his going north to Monterey. We can't let him travel alone. You are the logical one to take him home, Ixtil, but I don't command it. Ysaga and the children need you, too."

Ixtil deliberated, "I have an idea about that, Father. Let me talk to Ysaga. Perhaps we can arrange it so that the whole family can come along this time, without disturbing Fr. Serra, perhaps even cheering him up. By the way, Father, can you spare us four mules?"

"Seguramente, Ixtil. Take as many as you need."

"Four will do, I think. One for the *Presidente,* carrying his medicines in one saddlebag, his Mass necessities in the other. One for Ysaga, with Chiquita on her lap. One for me, with the food for us all. And a fourth for Ponce and Juan."

Fr. Joseph looked doubtful. "How can you keep two active boys on one unlucky mule?"

"Leave that to me," Ixtil said. "I am stricken by an idea."

Next morning, after Fr. Serra had confirmed the fifteen new candidates in the church—all that the mission was able to present at short notice—Ixtil could be heard in the carpenter shop, sawing and hammering. He emerged in the afternoon with two commodious boxes, without lids but connected by adjustable straps. At his call, Ysaga came to inspect them with great care; then climbed into one of them and sat in various positions.

"One for each of the boys to ride in," Ixtil explained. "The two boxes to be connected and made firm by straps under the mule's belly and over its back. Since Juan and Ponce are of almost equal weight, there will be no imbalance. What do you think, *cara?*"

"Chiquita will ride on my lap, so that she can suck whenever she is hungry?"

"Yes."

"The boxes are certainly large enough," Ysaga looked them over critically once more. "The children will squirm, inevitably, and maybe try to jump out, but a whack or two on their bottoms will convince them." She looked slyly at Ixtil. "The whacking is yours to do, husband."

"Who else?" he asked with a laugh. "You never spank them. If I didn't, they would grow up to be like wild beasts in the woods. You are too tender-hearted, *cara.*"

She shurgged. "In a mother, better than too hard-hearted, I think. Besides, I will take six blankets. Three in each saddlebox will render them soft and comfortable. Perhaps they can persuade the boys to sleep.''

Ixtil nodded approval. "In that way we should have a reasonably smooth trip."

"If the *Padre Presidente* can endure the riding," Ysaga added.

"There's always that, of course," Ixtil agreed, "but I've noticed that when he sets his will on some result he always gets it. He is determined to sleep in his own bed in his own mission. He will get there."

Three days later, Fr. Serra declared himself thoroughly rested and better than ready for the ride ahead. Early on the following morning, all were in good spirits. Ysaga's striplings occasioned much merriment when they settled into their nests on either side of the mission's gentlest mule. After seeing them in, and Ysaga on her mule, Ixtil lifted Chiquita into her arms. Then he helped the *Presidente* into the saddle of his mule and once more checked the medicines and religious articles in the priest's saddlebags, as well as the food packed into his own. Then farewells were shouted to and from the mission Chumash and their brown-robed friars.

Traveling with frequent stops, they reached by sundown, the summit of the Cuesta Trail, where they camped for the night. As always, Fr. Serra said the simple prayers before and after eating, and before they retired to sleep. Soon after daybreak, the children woke everybody up, running around, collecting firewood, and calling to one another in their high voices.

Ixtil and his family had slept deeply all night, but Fr. Serra, it appeared, had not. When Ixtil went to him to apologize and to see how he was, Fr. Serra laughed.

"It's much more likely," he said, "that I woke your youngsters than that they woke me. I do not need much sleep any more. I've been lying here for a long time, saying my prayers and meditating about their meaning. Also, alas, thinking of the administrative duties which await me at Monterey. Governor Neve will be back soon from the south. I've been trying in vain to forgive him, not for his injuries to me, which do not matter, but for his impediments to our missions, which matter a great deal."

He lay silent for a time. "Forgive the man, if not the deed. But what if the man is hopelessly entangled with his evil deeds? What then, Ixtil, what then?" Receiving no answer, he sighed deeply.

"It is all very difficult. Some say this religion of ours is simple enough. You pray for grace to do what you should. You receive it. Then you do what you should. This makes it all a kind of easy syllogism. But between the praying and the acting—such struggle, so many defeats! How can people call any of this simple? It's anything but simple for me."

"Breakfast is nearly ready, Father," Ixtil said.

"Good, I could eat something."

"I'll bring it to you."

Fr. Serra struggled to sit up. "I'll come. I'm not an invalid."

"No, but you have a long day of travel ahead. You should not exert yourself until you have to."

The priest sank back with a rueful smile. "I suppose I should not. Lord, lend me patience."

By easy stages they traveled down the Salinas River, with late springtime poppies, buttercups, lupin, and mustard flowers massed on both sides of El Camino Real. Ysaga, letting the children run through the lovely meadows, led the family mules into the grass.

Fr. Serra followed, gaining health from all the

beauty. "How mighty is God, Ixtil, mighty over all the world, yet He cares for every petal of every flower and for the tiniest insect on it. Thank God I can pray that, Ixtil, really pray it! Anyone who can is never lost, but finds God and His Son."

They lost track of time. Nobody seemed sure of how long it took them to reach Mission San Antonio. Yet they were expected there, and many preparations had been made. The *comida* in the evening was sumptuous. Next day, the quadrangle was almost solid with *Indios* who had gathered to receive confirmation from the *Padre Presidente*. The priests had been scouring all the villages for miles around, Ixtil reflected, just as he had helped to do in Mission San Luis Obispo.

Taking the *Indios* in groups of one hundred, with intervals of rest between, Fr. Serra spent two long days in giving the sacrament of confirmation to all who wished it. On the third day, a few more wandered in. Like the latecoming workers in the vineyard, as related in the parable of Our Lord, they received as much as those who came earliest—the sacrament fully bestowed with utmost care by the *Padre* who held the *patente*.

But the three days took their toll of his strength. The mission priests had to confine him to bed, despite his protests, in order that he might recover. Only at the end of a week did they judge him strong enough to ride his mule without torment, but Ixtil had to lift him into the saddle.

Near tears, Fr. Sitjar asked, "When will we see you again, Father?"

Fr. Serra laid a hand on his shoulder. "All lives end, Father; but, God willing, I will see you all once more, some time next year."

"We shall pray for that, Father."

"And for me, Buenaventura, please, I feel the need

for prayers."

The little group moved northward toward the *Presidente's* home mission. Again, from dawn to sunset they regaled themselves in timeless passage through the banks of fragrance and color which arrayed the meadows with a glory greater than Solomon's. They ate and slept under brilliant stars.

Fr. Serra lost the appearance of sickness, though not of age, and enjoyed play with the children. At times, they sat inside the circle of his arms while he told them eloquent stories from Scripture. At first, Ysaga watched these occasions with jealous eyes, but soon she was won by them utterly. She became both nurse and mother to the ailing old man, preparing simple foods, tastefully cooked, as she would have done for one of her own children, changing the bandages on his swollen leg, and driving everybody away when he needed rest. This regime continued after their arrival at Mission San Carlos, until Fr. Serra asked Ixtil with wonder, "How can she do so much for me without neglecting the children?"

"You do not know women, Father. Where they love they can do everything."

Ixtil had not taken his party through Monterey in reaching the mission on the bluff above the Rio Carmelo but had cut off from El Camino by a shorter route through the pinewoods. He did not want his invalid to face an encounter with Neve, if the Governor had returned to Monterey.

The news of Fr. Serra's return spread within a few hours, however, as *Indios* from the mission went into town to do day labor for the richer settlers or simply gossip with their friends at the *presidio* church. Many came, and not all were *Indios,* to welcome Fr. Serra and ask his blessing, which the priest gave willingly while reclining in his *sala* on a piece of home-made furniture, half couch, half bed. They kept coming until Ysaga drove them back, telling them that Father needed to eat his *comida* in peace. They should return in two or three days, after he had secured some rest from the labors of his long journey.

Neve was not among them. Ixtil passed to Fr. Serra the report, being whispered around Monterey, that Neve would return to the capital only to collect his personal effects. He had been transferred to the staff of Teodoro de Croix as a military captain. In his place as Governor, before the end of the year 1782, would appear the familiar figure of Pedro Fages, who had done well in frontier wars farther to the east and was being given another chance as Governor of California.

The report turned out to be true. One day, soon after the summer solstice, Neve rode with his escort into the mission compound and strode, with great jangling of spurs, into Fr. Serra's study, where Ixtil was trying to get down on paper, before he forgot it, a letter from Fr. Serra to the Commander of the Internal Provinces, Teodoro de Croix.

After coolly glancing at the name of the letter's addressee, Neve said to Fr. Serra, "I suppose you are wrecking my character, piece by piece, with my new employers." But mischief twinkled in his eyes.

"No, I am not, *Señor*. What sort of man, much less priest, would I be if I hurt you behind your back, whatever my opinion may be? No, the General has requested, as he has every right to do, an enumeration of our California missions already founded, their location on an accurate map, and a tally of *Indios,* priests, and Spanish civilians at each one. Also, each mission's crops for the past two years, the number and the species of its livestock, and so on. A thorough analysis. Your name is not mentioned here, nor is any matter of disagreement between us. Isn't that so, Ixtil?"

"It is so, *Padre.*"

"But you are defending the Franciscan mission system." Neve's tone of voice made it less a question than a statement.

"Of course, *Señor.* I and my priests believe in it. Moreover, it is under challenge by a Bishop Reyes, who thinks it breeds disobedience among missionaries and causes us to force our *Indios* to work like slaves."

"Reyes? Reyes?" Neve looked puzzled. "I do not know him."

"I am glad to hear that, *Señor,* since some of his conceptions of what a mission ought to be resemble yours," Fr. Serra said. "This Reyes has managed to persuade the King to make him Bishop over Sonora, Sinaloa, and both Californias."

Neve laughed. "You thought he and I might be working together to destroy your precious Franciscan system, I suppose?"

"Yes, *Señor,* I did."

"What, exactly, does this Bishop Reyes propose, *Padre Presidente?*"

"In each of his four provinces a central 'custody' or convent of the missionaries working in that province. They are to be sent out as needed to preach here and there, presumably over some regular route, but not to live with their *Indios.* They live only in the 'custody,' where each priest is controlled directly by the Bishop, and by him alone. Franciscans, Dominicans, Augustinians, and the others—all live together without distinction of order and without being subject to their mother houses in Ciudad de Mexico or anywhere else. There is much more, but that is enough to give you a sample."

"It is indeed." Neve drew a deep breath. *"Padre*

Presidente, I am not an irreligious man, though you may think so. Nor do I altogether dislike the missions founded by you Franciscans. Your system seems to me to work well in wildernesses far from towns. But when the missions are near *pueblos* or *presidios,* their good should take second place to the good of the *gente de razon* in such towns and military bases. The citizens and soldiers who live in them have souls to save, too. Now, they are also the chief population of this country of California. To them, not to the Indians, you priests owe your first obligations.

"Incidentally, I favor maintaining the differences between the various types of orders, and keeping them hierarchically organized, as our whole Church is."

Fr. Serra nodded his head. *"Señor,* I wish we could have had this talk years ago, when you first came here as Governor. We should all have understood one another better, and worked together more smoothly. For me, at least, it is too late."

Neve smiled, a genuine smile. "I know you are unwell, Father. I have tired you, I fear. Watch over your health. *Vaya con Dios."*

"Con Dios," said Fr. Serra, blessing him. The jingling of Neve's spurs diminished, then fell completely silent, and were replaced by the sound of horses being mounted and galloped away.

Fr. Serra sighed, "Ah, Ixtil, this life of ours is full of farewells, and missed opportunities. I blame myself for not conciliating that man. He has a softer side, and ideas of his own which need not have hurt us missionaries as much as we thought."

"I have hated him myself, *Padre.* Now I discover that I need not have."

Fr. Serra regarded Ixtil with affection. "We both erred. Now let us be sure not to err again with the

new Governor Fages. You and I found much to like,
and to dislike, in him during his first term. And I
went all the way to Ciudad de Mexico to ask the
Viceroy to transfer him away from us. That is past—
all past. I hope Fages will not look backward to old
quarrels but forward to a time without them. When
does he arrive?''

"In about six weeks, they say."

"Muy bien. This leg of mine should be better then.''

"Better, but not well," Ysaga told Ixtil that night
after the children had been put to bed in their room
with the three bunks.

"How do you diagnose his malady?" Ixtil asked her.

"You know I am no doctor, *querido,* but I notice
the leg sometimes has fever, sometimes not. The sickness is far inside, maybe in the bone. The older he
gets, the more easily it conquers his body. He is
aging fast now. He will never be wholly well again,
I think."

"How much longer ought we to stay here, then?"

"It is for you to decide. You are helping him greatly
with his many papers, and you two like to talk together. As for me, I like to tend to him. To me, he
is more fatherlike than my physical father. On the
other hand, the children do not prosper here. The
climate is too cold, with foggy wind always blowing
from the sea. One or another seems always to be a
little sick, with aching ears."

Ixtil pondered. "The children are not used to it."

"Yes," Ysaga agreed, "but do not send us home
to good Fr. Joseph, while you work here. Whatever
we do, let it be done together."

"I am lucky to have such a good wife, Ysaga. Suppose we wait until Governor Fages arrives. If Fr.
Serra and he agree well together, we will leave a few

days later."

"So be it, Ixtil, my good husband."

Gradually their lives settled into a routine. In the afternoons Ixtil helped the *Padre Presidente* with his interrogatories, which multiplied. With every ship came another pile of them. Each required five copies: one for Fr. Serra's files, one each for the Mother House and the Viceroy, one for the Governor, and one for De Croix as Commander of the Internal Provinces.

"We waste much paper here," Fr. Serra would say, surveying with distaste the orderly files of reports on his big table, on his chairs, on his cold floors next to the walls. "The recipients, if they read all these replies to their questions, know more about the state of the missions than we ourselves. Their curiosity increases in direct proportion to their distance from us."

"Give me a *permiso, Padre,* and I will have shelves manufactured for you," Ixtil offered. But they were filled with files on the very day the carpenter delivered them. Soon the papers were expanding again, filling all their former positions on table, chairs, and floor.

"I feel like turning arsonist," Ixtil remarked disgustedly. "A fire could do much good in this room."

In the mornings he contributed his labor to the mission farms some miles up the Rio Carmelo, where the sun drank up the ocean fogs and most grains and tubers grew well. Often he took his two boys with him, freeing Ysaga's hands for the baby and for Fr. Serra's infected leg. The lads were just old enough to play at farming, without hurting the crops as they grew.

In the early autumn, Governor Fages came to Monterey and assumed his office. Ixtil took him a note from Fr. Serra, inviting him to call at Mission San Carlos when he had time. On the following Saturday,

Fages rode to the mission and found the *Padre Presidente* limping happily among the flowers of his garden.

After a moment of hesitation, the two men opened their arms and gave each other the *abrazo.* "It is good, *Señor Padre Presidente,* to see you out of your bed, where you have spent so much time lately. How goes the leg?"

"As God wills, as God wills," replied the priest. "I cannot walk very far yet, but at least I can walk. In your honor, Excellency, for this is the first morning of my arising. Somewhat like Lazarus, eh?"

"Not like him, I hope. Of course, death is always close to every one of us, but I trust that yours is many years away. We need you here, *Padre,* for the good of our souls."

Fr. Serra gestured toward a stone bench nearby and both men sat down.

"I have come to make my peace with you, *Padre.* In the past I have been unbearable, both in my actions and in my failures to act. I intend to be bearable from now on—with God's help, of course."

Fr. Serra rubbed his sore leg automatically as he listened and then spoke.

"You will find me very easy to make peace with, *Señor* Fages. In fact, I planned to come to Monterey this afternoon to make the same request of you. I do not feel happy about my past. What man does? But especially with you, *Señor,* I am haunted by thoughts of how I might have acted, not only with more charity but with more justice. Shall we forgive each other, and ourselves?"

"To my very great content, *Padre.*" Fages paused with delicacy. "It is very well known how you were humiliated at Santa Barbara last year. I would be glad to make reparation by founding the mission there whenever you wish. We could also establish Mission

Purísima to the west, if you like, while we are in that region."

Fr. Serra glowered at his lame leg so intently that he seemed bent on healing it with a look.

"This is most handsome of you, *Señor,* most handsome, and under ordinary circumstances I would fly to accept. But now my weakness of body stands in the way. I rather think it will allow me only one more journey of any length. I have a choice between founding those two missions you mention or visiting all my missions for the last time, to give the sacrament of confirmation to the baptized *Indios* who have not yet received it."

He paused for a long thought. "I now decide in favor of the journey of confirmations. Next spring I shall go by ship to San Diego and come back north on muleback, mission by mission, strengthening with the sacrament of the Holy Spirit those who are due to receive it. If, after that, my body allows me to found the other two channel missions, I shall

Chapter 15

The soldier and the priest parted on such cordial terms that Ixtil decided he could return with his family to Mission San Luis Obispo the following week. Among the local *Indios,* Ysaga found a faithful woman whom she taught how to cook for Father and, particularly, how to make his infected leg more comfortable.

Fr. Serra listened to this process with much amusement.

"You should hear how voluble the two of them are," he told Ixtil, "and how meticulous. Each keeps correcting the other, as if this old carcass of mine were a most precious object, to be cared for properly only as she prescribes."

"They love you, Father. Doesn't that great fact compensate for all the fuss they are making? Or would you rather that they become more tranquil—and more careless?"

"More tranquil," said the priest. "In a woman, tranquillity is the cardinal virtue."

"You do not know women, Father."

"What! After all my hours in the confessional?"

"And after all my years of living intimately with one?"

Both men laughed. But they were close to tears when Ixtil led his little procession southward to El Camino. Fr. Serra had given his own riding mule for Ysaga and the little girl. The two boys, in their balanced packing cases, munched candied fruits from Spain. Ixtil and Ysaga wore jade crucifixes, beautifully carved by a native craftsman and just blessed by the *Padre Presidente* himself.

"Next year, we hope!" Ixtil called out, above the shrill voices of his family.

"God, and my body, willing!" came the answering farewell.

Though broken by an overnight stop at Mission San Antonio, the journey home was short and pleasant. Before they knew it, they were riding down the Cuesta trail and into the patio of Mission San Luis Obispo, where they were greeted by Fr. Joseph with a *"Hola!* Welcome home, you wanderers!" All their friends, it seemed, had turned out to greet them. There was a loud commotion everywhere.

Ysaga wanted to get back to their house with all speed, and did so, but Fr. Joseph detained Ixtil to learn all the news about Monterey and the other missions, now nine in number. The two men sat on a bench among the flowers in the patio. The questions began with "How did you leave Fr. Serra?" and ended with "Did you see Governor Fages?"

Long before Ixtil had answered them all, he also found himself addressing a crowd of his people who had gradually joined themselves to his audience. They squeezed him dry of information before they let him go.

After supper, Fr. Joseph walked to Ixtil's house to speak of matters he had preferred not to display publicly earlier in the day.

"You remember," he said, "that before you left we were preparing for the election of an *alcalde* and two assistants through whom the *Indios* can govern themselves in this mission, under the guidance of myself and my associate clergy. All this has been in accord with the new regulations for all the missions decreed by the Viceroy. Theoretically, this is just. The trouble is that our *alcalde* has just run away with the wife of another man, probably into the mountains of the interior. We can get along nicely without that rascal, but in his place we must elect another *alcalde*, an honest one this time.''

Ixtil nodded. ''I remember the correspondence. You appealed to Fr. Serra, and he to Governor Neve, but nobody could do anything. The rules are incomplete because they exempt the *alcalde* from discipline for faults he commits while in office.''

''Just so,'' agreed the priest. ''But wherever the defect lies, we still must elect a new *alcalde*. Will you offer yourself as a candidate, Ixtil?''

Ixtil looked forward into the life of an *alcalde* and did not like what he saw. To act as a combination mayor and justice of the peace! It would be a tangle of troubles. All he wanted was peace at home with Ysaga and the children.

''Please, Ixtil,'' urged Fr. Cavaller, his teacher and friend, to whom he owed everything.

Ixtil hesitated before saying reluctantly, ''If I must, I must.''

''Good. Thank God, and thank you. I know how much I ask of you, but the fact is that I really trust no other. Enough of that, for the time being. Now for another matter of more general concern.

''My country, Spain, is at war with another country, England, and war is always expensive. Weapons, horses, uniforms, ships, additional food for the soldiers, money for their pay—all are required, besides other things never foreseen.

''So each mission is assessed a sum of money for the war. We at San Luis Obispo have been assessed $107, which we must pay. But, like all the other missions, we have no money as such—no coins, no silver, no gold; only livestock and crops. So we must sell these for money. On this continent our only markets with money are the *pueblos* and the *presidios* at San Diego, Monterey, and San Francisco. Consequently, we are sending some of our cattle, sheep, pigs, and horses—and some of our wheat seed, corn, and beans—to the *presidio* at San Diego, which will sell all it can to the *pueblos* and ship the remainder to Mexico for sale there."

"It is a great drain for the mission," Ixtil said, looking grave. "But, even worse, it will seem unjust to our *Indios,* who work to produce these crops and livestock, only to see them disappear without bringing any return."

"Every word you say is true," Fr. Joseph admitted. "War is a devourer. But if a people does not defend itself, its enemies eat it up. You have seen the results of raids by inland savages against your peaceful villages along the channel."

Ixtil had only one question. "Is the parallel between our tribal wars and your national wars exact?"

"Not exact in every detail, but in its main outlines, yes. This is my own opinion, of course."

"Then," said Ixtil, "we must help your country, which has helped us."

Lying awake that night, Fr. Joseph searched his conscience to find whether he might have deceived Ixtil, but decided he had not. Being a Spanish patroit far from home, he believed in his country, and found good reasons for seeing it as more sinned against than sinning.

Ixtil easily won the election as *alcalde.* Although he had been away from Mission San Luis Obispo a good deal, he was generally liked for his friendliness. Even his absences from the mission helped his case because they involved him in what his people recognized as great issues. Nor was he unduly linked with the soldiers locally and elsewhere, who were the least trusted, and often the worst hated, of the Spaniards.

From the start of his tenure he kept working with the agriculture in all its stages, and with the care and riding of the horses. He did not want to be considered solely as an official but, at least partly, as a fellow worker who did his share of the physical labor and sweated his share of the sweat.

The morning hours just after Mass were the times when he heard charges of breaches of the peace, petty theft, disputes over precedence, complaints about the quality or quantity of the foods served in the communal kitchen or distributed to families for preparation and eating in the privacy of their huts, the justice or injustice of labor assignments, and other types of minor offences inevitable among the many hundreds living at the mission. The few major crimes and sins he left strictly to the supreme authority of the priests and, likewise, charges by *Indios* against the five soldiers of the garrison. His judgments were limited to restitution, wherever possible, or to light sentences of imprisonment in the mission jail. On occasion, he decreed a short sitting in the public stocks, but only for men. If women sat in the stocks, they did so in the *monjerio,* where the matron in charge could see that infractions against modesty and decency did not occur.

To begin, Ixtil aimed at reforms in only two areas of the life of his people. In one of these, food, he persuaded Fr. Joseph to slaughter at least one or two cattle every few weeks in order that meat should be added to the constant round of *atole* and *posole,* which constituted the staple diet of the Chumash. The persuasion was not hard, because the mission now had over 700 cattle, increasing yearly. Already the *vaqueros* had moved the herd over the hump of

El Monte to La Laguna, where the animals had water
and grass in abundance. They had also set up a hut
there so that one of the men could always keep an
eye out for marauders. Actually, Ixtil found, the
Chumash came to prefer the flesh of horses and
mules to any other, but the herds of these creatures
were still small, and precious for other uses.

A more difficult reform consisted in teaching the
people what diseases were contagious, according to
La Medicina Domestica, and in quarantining all who
had such evils in their bodies. To this end, Fr. Joseph
ordered the addition of two big rooms to the hospital,
entered through separate doors and not open to the
rest of the building. Ixtil and the priest taught Ysaga
how to recognize the sickness of the male and female
parts of the body. Ysaga then taught the nurses at
the hospital and the matron of the *monjerio* how to
examine the women, while Fr. Joseph and Ixtil taught
the two male nurses how to do the same for the men.
Many a time Ixtil thanked the good *Jesu* that De Anza
had revealed to him such a diagnosis. To be sure,
most of the patients of this kind died anyway, but at
least it was without further infecting others.

The campo santo around the church kept filling,
but a little more slowly.

About this time, Ixtil found that Fr. Joseph had to
draw up an *informe* answering many questions about
the affairs of his mission, every year. It was necessary
to report how many beasts, and of what species,
belonged to the mission. Since the herds were now
ranging freely, under the guidance of their herdsmen,
wherever forage was most plentiful at each season,
the final compilations were not easy to arrive at.
The *informes* also wanted to know how many *Indios*
were alive that year, how many had died, or married,
or had children, and of these how many were baptized.

As if Fr. Joseph would allow anyone to be born or to die on mission ground without the proper ceremonies!

Helping to prepare all these answers, Ixtil realized that the reports of the numbers from every mission all went to Fr. Serra and that these were the papers he had helped the *Padre Presidente* copy and recopy, and finally total up. Nine missions, so far! Small wonder that the *Presidente* found such labor a heavy burden and wished he were not *presidente* of anything. Yet when he weighed the good with the bad, Ixtil saw why the great ones in the government at Ciudad de Mexico, who had spent so much money and so many lives in sending the missionaries and their supplies to California, would wish to know what were the returns to themselves and to *el Dios bueno*. And how much more might yet be asked of them!

A vision of the whole enterprise, with all its needs, clarified itself in Ixtil's mind. It was, certainly, a mighty work.

In these labors passed the year belonging to God in which Ixtil was *alcalde*. Whether he should stand for election again began to be discussed by the priests and by his own people. Little opposition showed itself, but before Ixtil's term was up, a courier brought a letter from Fr. Serra at Mission San Diego, addressed to Fr. Joseph.

Written in the season of falling leaves in the year of Our Lord 1783, it explained that Fr. Serra had sailed from Monterey to San Diego and was slowly moving northward from mission to mission in order to bestow the sacrament of confirmation once more.

The less said about the condition of my leg the better, but at least I can still ride a mule. Brothers and friends, gather your people who need the sacrament so that I

may miss no soul. A cloud gathers over us Franciscans,
and who knows what may happen? Of this I shall speak
when I see you. How are Ixtil and his family, who were
so kind to me last year? Tell them I miss them sorely.

Always in Christ,
Fr. Junipero Serra

"He never complains of his leg," said Ixtil sadly.
"It must be very bad now." He thought silently before
he spoke again. "Fr. Joseph, if you will release me
from offering myself for another term as *alcalde,* and
if Ysaga agrees, I should like to help him get back
home to Mission San Carlos, as we did last year."

"Of course; since he needs you, you must go. His
letter virtually asks that you accompany him. We shall
miss you, though."

"Not so much, Father, if my two *regidores* and I see
to it, first, that those of my people who need confirmation are assembled here before the *Padre Presidente*
arrives. I'm becoming pretty expert at this, you know."
Ixtil smiled. "Will you give me the authority to arrange
the ingathering?"

"Gratefully, my Ixtil. It's in your hands."

Ixtil, his *regidores,* and the elders of each village
wrought so well that eighty-eight candidates were waiting when Fr. Serra at last arrived on muleback, accompanied by two mounted soldiers. One look at the aged
and feeble *Presidente* told Ixtil of his condition, as
he took the old man in his arms and carefully lifted
him down. Finding that Fr. Serra could scarcely stand,
much less walk, he carried his light body to the bed
prepared for him in the priests' house. There Ysaga
ministered to his leg and to his other needs, as she
had in the past, every gentle movement expressing
her love and reverence.

As she and Ixtil left the *Presidente* to his rest, Ysaga,

who had been undecided whether to go north with him, told Ixtil, "I must certainly go with you. The children will be safe with Consuela, especially if Fr. Joseph will keep an eye on them, too."

"I'm glad," said Ixtil, pressing her arm.

That night Fr. Serra, much refreshed, was able to sit down to supper without too much discomfort. When the meal was over, he sent for Ixtil and his wife to take part in the discussion which was about to begin. On arriving, they found at the priests' table not only Fr. Cavaller and Fr. Paterna but also Fr. Buenaventura Sitjar, who had come the distance from Mission San Antonio to help in any way he could.

Fr. Serra welcomed the couple warmly, and had two chairs pulled up to the table for them, but lost no time in getting down to business.

"You remember, Joseph, the hint about bad news which I dropped in my letter?"

"Seguramente," said Fr. Cavaller. "In fact, you've had us worried to death."

"Then let me remove the worry without more delay and supply the facts, which are sufficiently troublesome in their own right. You all know, I think, Fr. Hidalgo, *Presidente* of the Dominicans in Baja California. Well, I have been astonished to learn that he has applied for permission to abandon those miserable missions down there and to take over our prosperous missions up here, in Alta."

"But this is incredible!" cried Fr. Paterna. "After all our labors here, since '69?"

"Fr. Hidalgo has always been an ambitious man," said Fr. Serra mildly.

"And greedy," added Fr. Sitjar. "How did he make this application, *Padre Presidente?"*

"Through Bishop Reyes. He persuaded the Bishop to write letters to the Commander of the Provincias

Internas, proposing the change."

"Ah, Reyes! Our most stupid and wayward Bishop, the inventor of the local "custodies' of unhappy memory. And how have Teodoro de Croix and his Lt. Neve responded?"

"So far, not at all, Buenaventura. Which I take to be a sign of hope."

Fr. Joseph lifted an eyebrow. "Of hope, Father? After the way Neve treated you when he was Governor?"

Fr. Serra agreed somberly: "Not well, Joseph, not well. I have an excellent memory of my encounters with him. But just before he left Monterey to join De Croix, we had a talk which showed him in a better light. You did not hear that meeting, Joseph." He brightened. "He spoke like a good Christian. So I have hope."

Fr. Sitjar mused aloud. "If priests could wager, I would wager that I know the lever Fr. Hidalgo is using to oust us. To wit, an agreement not to continue the Franciscan mission system here but to go back to the parish church idea—under Bishop Reyes, of course. In this conception the *Indios* do not live and work communally at the church but remain in their *rancherias,* to which the priest rides out on his mule to teach and help them. Only on Sundays do the *Indios* walk to the church to hear Mass—if they feel like making the effort. You remember how it worked, or rather failed to work, when we tried it ourselves in Baja."

Fr. Serra sighed. "Such a system loses too many souls. I will write to De Croix and Neve, humbling myself and begging them to let us finish our work here. Also to our Mother House and to the Viceroy. Somehow they must hear us! I will pray an extra rosary each day for a year, asking the Blessed Virgin to intercede for us."

The other priests made a similar resolve. Later, Ixtil went with them into the church to follow the Stations of the Cross.

Next day, making a supreme effort, the *Padre Presidente* confirmed the eighty-eight communicants whom Fr. Cavaller presented for confirmation.

He stayed two days in bed afterward to acquire strength for the continuance of his journey northward. Then, when Ixtil had lifted him into the saddle of his mule, he was able to keep his seat and ride off, up the road toward Monterey.

The journey to Monterey dazed Ixtil and Ysaga at first. To Ixtil, the lifting on and off to procure rest seemed to go on all day, so frequent were the stops. Even when Fr. Serra rode, he often had to be supported by Ixtil and Ysaga, propping him up from either side. For long periods the priest said nothing, though they could see his lips moving in prayer. When he spoke to them, his mind seemed to be wandering somewhere between the past and the present. Occasionally Fr. Serra regained control, and at such times he spoke eloquently about death and its Christian meaning. They listened to him as if enchanted by some spell in his voice.

"Death is not important," he would say. "What matters is our state of mind when we die. Do we love God enough? If so, He receives us as disobedient children reclaimed. If not, He can reject." Then he would mutter to himself before continuing. "Yet can we sinners ever love Him enough? O my sins, my many and heavy sins! Can He forgive so many?"

During other conscious moments he told his beads, also saying the additional rosary he had vowed, beseeching the Virgin's intercession to help the Franciscans stay in California. Then the comas returned, and the senseless mutterings which accompanied them.

"Is he dying?" Ixtil asked Ysaga.

"He has much fever from the poison in his leg, but I don't think so," she replied.

Many times each day she bathed the leg in cool water, stroked it gently, and applied fresh bandages. Then they rode on again.

Fr. Sitjar had ridden ahead to warn those of Mission San Antonio that Fr. Serra was at hand, and very ill. When the *Padre Presidente* rode up to the entrance of the mission patio, a comfortable bed awaited him, strengthening foods, and all possible tender care. With miraculous vital power, he was able to sit all the following morning on a chair in front of the altar, confirming the many dozens of *Indios* who crowded into the little church.

"No more, Buenaventura?" he asked wistfully, at the end.

"Not even one more, *Padre Presidente*," answered Fr. Sitjar. "And now I must take you back to bed."

"When we are old," Fr. Serra quoted sadly, "others take us where we would not go." But he submitted to Fr. Sitjar's order.

After half a week of rest he was able to sit astride his mule and to ride with Ixtil and Ysaga on the last lap home to Carmel Valley. As he sank down on his bed in his own room, he prayed aloud in gratitude: "Lord, I thank Thee for my journey, profitable to so many souls, and for my safe return home. Bless especially, dear Lord, your servants Ixtil and Ysaga, who have relieved my misery of body by taking much of it into themselves."

He looked fondly at Ysaga. "When will you be taking that husband of your back to San Luis Obispo, your dearest mission?"

She finished taking his pulse before she said, "As

soon as I can be sure that you will be getting good care from those who are here. Not a moment sooner.''

"My Martha," murmured the priest with a smile.

After a week of demonstration and supervision, Ysaga expressed her approval of Fr. Serra's attendants and her readiness to leave. When she and Ixtil went to say good-bye to the priest, Fr. Serra said to them, "I don't know whether we shall meet again this side of heaven."

"Nonsense!" Ysaga exclaimed. "You, with your so great vitality, like a fountain always rushing up from below! You will live for many a year yet."

"It all belongs to God," said Fr. Serra. "Shall we leave it with Him?"

He blessed them solemnly before they left.

Chapter 16

"I doubt that he will live another year," Ixtil told his wife.

"So do I," she replied, "but it might have done harm to say so."

"When my time comes," said Ixtil, "I hope I may die with half the faith and courage he is displaying."

Ixtil reached Mission San Luis Obispo in time to be reelected *alcalde* for another year, but he did not hurry his arrival for that purpose. He did not particularly want to wield the limited power to judge and to punish his fellow Chumash, which the office of *alcalde* conferred. He would rather be merely one of them, not made superior to them by an office of any kind. He began to think that the superior position disturbed his worship of *el Dios bueno*.

Ixtil consulted Fr. Joseph about this trouble, but was surprised to find that the priest disagreed with him strongly. "You *Indios* need some self-rule," he said. "Your race selected you to help rule it."

"I don't understand," said Ixtil. "I am not the self of my race. I am only Ixtil."

"Yet, being elected to office by your race, you become the self of your race, but only for the purposes of that office."

Ixtil puzzled over the unfamiliar words. "You mean I become two selves, an Ixtil self and a Chumash self?"

"Something like that."

"But, Father," Ixtil persisted, "the two selves get mixed up together and destroy each other."

"Then you must keep them separate. Whenever you do the work of an *alcalde* you are the Chumash self. At all other times you are your Ixtil self."

"But Father, that is impossible!" Ixtil exclaimed. "When I am my Chumash self everybody still remembers, and I myself still remember, that I am only Ixtil pretending to be more important than Ixtil. And when as my Ixtil self I walk across the patio to do something for Ysaga and the children, nobody forgets that I am *alcalde*."

"I see I have been too metaphysical. What it comes down to is this: A good, private Ixtil self can mix with a good public Chumash self, provided always that both are good. In fact, they make each other better."

"I see," said Ixtil slowly, but he didn't, quite. "Suppose," he said, "the public self stains the holiness of the private self?"

"Is that happening?" asked Fr. Joseph. "No, of course not. You come to Mass regularly, confess in the confessional, and give much of your work to the church."

"It is an interior thing, Father."

The priest pondered. "If the *alcalde* self is truly hurting the sincerity of your religion, that is very bad, and you must stop being *alcalde*. But that need not happen. Remember, Ixtil, that *Jesu* led both a public and private life. He wants the Christian life to be both internal and external—internal in its private search for God, external in its attempts to help other people. Does my being a priest who tries to help *Indios* in their daily lives harm my adoration of *Jesu, Maria y José?*"

Now Ixtil saw. "Of course not, Father. You would

not be a priest if you were holy only for yourself."

"Exactly. And you would not be a good Christian unless, being holy in yourself, you tried to help others to live Christian lives also."

In berry-picking time in the year belonging to God, 1784, a courier brought two letters from Monterey for Fr. Joseph. The first one announced Fr. Serra's death a few days earlier. After reading it slowly, Fr. Joseph handed the letter without comment to Ixtil, who was transcribing one of the annual *informes*.

Ixtil could scarcely believe that Fr. Serra's strong, luminous voice would never again be heard on this earth.

"Fr. Serra dead!" he exclaimed, brushing tears from his eyes. He felt Fr. Joseph's hand on his shoulder.

"No need to grieve, my Ixtil. Death was a release for that saintly soul, long bound to a suffering body. He is safe in heaven now, I think."

Ixtil pulled himself together. "A high requiem Mass for him tomorrow morning, Father?"

"Indeed yes." Fr. Joseph reflected for a moment. "Would it not be strange if we, who pray *for* him now, would be praying *to* San Junipero in the years to come?"

Fr. Joseph opened the other letter, a copy of one written by Commander Neve of the Internal Provinces to Bishop Reyes. "It appears," he said as he read, "that Fr. Serra was justified in his hope that Neve has become a different man since leaving the governorship of California. Our rosaries have been successful. We underestimate Mary's power. Here, read."

Ixtil could hardly credit what he read. Neve's reply to Bishop Reyes' letters on behalf of the Dominicans who coveted the California missions was, in effect, a sharp rebuke. Neve praised the achievements of the

Franciscans in these missions. Moreover, he stressed that the Dominicans had displayed no great success in their establishments in Baja California.

"I wonder whether the *Padre Presidente* received this before he died."

Fr. Joseph studied the dates on both letters. "I think not. This copy of Neve's letter appears to have reached Mission San Carlos after Fr. Serra's death. He died thinking that all his work in California would fall into Dominican hands. But God did not wish it so. Call Fr. Paterna, Ixtil, if you please."

Fr. Paterna read the letters eagerly but said only: "What a strange mixture of sorrow and rejoicing can come in the same courier's pouch! So we don't get thrown out of California after all."

"No, Antonio, not now and not ever, I think, unless we Spaniards lose our New World territories, especially Mexico. By the way, have you thought about who is to be Fr. Serra's successor? Have you any idea at all?"

"None really," replied Fr. Paterna. "It is well known, though, that Fr. Serra was grooming Fr. Fermin de Lasuén to take his place. What do you think of him?"

Fr. Joseph hesitated too long. "What *should* I think of him? He is a Franciscan priest like me. I do not gossip about my fellow priests."

Fr. Paterna laughed. "Ah, the good Joseph who speaks no evil. Have you no doubts at all?"

"A few, perhaps."

"Well, I have many," said Fr. Paterna in his outspoken way. "When he first arrived in California he showed signs of discontent with his lot as a missionary. Governor Rivera wanted him as his personal chaplain, and he was most willing. Our Mother House, though, objected that it could not supply anybody with a private confessor. A personal chaplain, mind you! In that episode he showed a high opinion of himself. But since then he seems to have developed some self-knowledge and, as report goes, is well enough liked by those who have worked with him. All seem to agree that he is an able administrator."

"You encourage me, Antonio."

"Wait until you see him in action as *Padre Presidente,* after having Fr. Serra."

Fr. Joseph nodded. "That may be sooner than you think. He will be passing through here before long, coming down from Carmel to inspect some sites for two missions on the channel coast which Fr. Serra left uncertain because of his conflict with Neve. Since then, Governor Fages has been exploring them and others in the neighborhood, and has recommended two locations to Fr. Lasuén. The latter is not the kind of man who takes the word of anybody else, even a Governor, in choosing anything so important as a location for a mission. He will go over the proposed areas inch by inch."

Ixtil held his peace but thought this a very necessary trait in a *Padre Presidente* of all the missions. Consequently, he was favorably disposed to Fr. Lasuén when the priest and the Governor rode in together one afternoon early in the year belonging to God, 1785.

The two men were almost direct contrasts. Fages was a restless, active, talkative, emotional sort whereas Fr. Lasuén was introspective, precise, self-controlled, and a master of the long, considering stare. Ixtil would have preferred a *Padre Presidente* somewhere between the two, but, as he said to himself, we must take what the Lord gives us and be thankful.

He could see that such a man as Fr. Lasuén would never need the help of an Ixtil. This view was confirmed when the priests did not invite him or Ysaga

to their table that evening, though they called him in
after the meal to clear away the dishes and pour the
wine. When he left, they had gathered around the
large maps of the channel, discussing possibilities.

Now began a period in Ixtil's life when he seldom
left his mission but concentrated on his growing family,
his duties as *alcalde,* inspections of the hospital and
monjerio, his stint at the agriculture and care for the
livestock, and his services as altar boy during Sunday
Masses. Nor could he quite escape the role of copyist
for Fr. Joseph when the *informes* became due, or when
an unexpected *interrogatorio* emerged from the brains
of some overzealous official far away in Ciudad de
Mexico.

The year belonging to God, 1786, marked itself into
memory as the year when Mission Santa Barbara came
into existence. Much traffic of men and wagons made
their noises along El Camino Real. Although most
of the heavy goods for Mission Santa Barbara came by
ship from Mexico, much arrived in wagons and on
pack mules from Monterey. The same held true for
its companion, the proposed *Mission La Purísima
Concepción de la Santísima Virgen Maria.*

Those at Mission San Luis Obispo heard first by
rumor and then by mail that Fr. Lasuén, having examined the proposed Montecito site for Mission Santa
Barbara, chose instead a spot known locally as El
Pedregoso (the Strong Place), closer to the *presido*—in
fact, only half a league away. There, on December 4,
1786, the feast day of Santa Barbara, virgin and
martyr, he raised and blessed a great cross. Governor
Fages being delayed, Fr. Lasuén waited courteously
until his arrival on December 14 before accomplishing
the formal rites of foundation for the mission. Fr.
Lasuén scratched from the *Presidio* books Fr. Serra's

"Mission and Royal *Presidio*" inscription and wrote instead: *"Esta Nueva Real Presidio,"* thus officially separating it from Mission Santa Barbara.

"A wrong righted at last!" said Fr. Paterna, rubbing his hands together. "But I wish Fr. Lasuén joy of the nearness of his mission to the Santa Barbara *presidio*. He deliberately moved the mission closer to the *presidio*, they say. That arrangement did not work at either San Diego or Monterey. No prophet is needed to foresee that it will not work at Santa Barbara either, unless both the mission and the *presidio* are populated with saints."

"Do not always see only the worst, Antonio," Fr. Joseph answered. "At least you must grant that our new *Padre Presidente* shows signs of being a man of action."

"So far, so good, Joseph. But why did he not go on to found Mission La Puŕisima a few miles to the west, as planned?"

Fr. Joseph smiled. "Well, I suppose because our Viceroy, having given to Mission Santa Barbara the 1,000 *pesos* needed to outfit each new mission, had no more to give. He has promised that the foundation money for Mission La Puŕisima will be given next year, allowing the mission to be built a few months later, but certainly in 1787. Doesn't that please you?"

"It will, when it is built."

Fr. Cavaller's voice was edged with impatience. "Can't you see, Antonio, that since Fr. Serra's death the growth of our chain of missions along the Santa Barbara coastline has resumed? Fr. Serra's last years expended themselves in fighting his disease and fighting Governor Neve on the confirmation dispute, while traveling up and down the province repeatedly to administer confirmation. Fighting, fighting, fighting. He had to do it, of course. But now all that is gone. I feel a forward movement."

He was right. Fr. Lasuén wrote to the priests of Mission San Luis Obispo asking whether they could spare for the dowry of Mission La Purísima at least fifty cattle, twenty mules, ten horses, half a dozen swine and a like number of sheep, together with any extra tools they might have for agriculture and carpentry. The Viceroy's 1,000 pesos had not yet arrived, but as soon as the money came, Mission San Luis Obispo would be repaid at current prices. The letter concluded by inviting whomever they cared to bring to witness the founding at Lompoc, not later than December 10.

"This is a sad development," Fr. Paterna grumbled, "eating up one mission to establish another, like a cannibal."

But Fr. Cavaller responded curtly, after conferring with Ixtil, that San Luis Obispo could make such a loan with only slight difficulty.

"If one Christian mission cannot trust another, who will ever trust it in time of need?"

"You have a point there, Joseph—you *do* have a point," Fr. Paterna said. "But suppose the central government discovers that it can found missions by this type of begging, from mission to mission; will it ever bother to dig into its own pockets for the 1,000 pesos it has given every new mission in the past?"

Fr. Joseph sighed. "That's true, too, Antonio. We must somehow establish the principle that if our central government will not support a new mission, then we old ones cannot do it, either."

This problem was to haunt Fr. Lasuén's nightmares when the Napoleonic Wars cut off the flow of funds from Spain in the next two decades. But in the autumn of 1787, when Mission La Purísima was to be founded, nobody dreamed of a Napoleon.

On the first day of December, Fr. Joseph, on muleback, led the train of livestock and other necessaries, bound for Lompoc. Ixtil and one of the *vaqueros* herded the cattle, mules, horses, sheep, and other animals while apprentices of the agriculture and carpentry looked after the mules bearing their precious instruments. Three days later, at the appointed site, they were greeted warmly not only by Fr. Lasuén himself but also by Fr. Fuster and Fr. Arroita. In addition, they met priests from Mission Santa Barbara and Mission San Buenaventura, each of them bringing contributions to the mission about to be born. In his thoughts, Ixtil wished Fr. Serra could be there to see his dream fulfilled.

On December 8, the Feast of the Immaculate Conception, Fr. Lasuén blessed the earth, air, and water, erected the cross, and named the foundation *La Mision de la Purísima Concepción de la Santísima Virgen, Madre de Dios y Nuestra Señora.* Carefully, he explained to the Indians who had come with the priests from the other missions that it meant the conception, in the womb of Mary's mother, *Santa Ana,* of a Virgin unspotted by original sin—and did not refer to Mary's conception of a sinless Christ. On an altar sheltered by brushwood, the priests concelebrated a high Mass.

Next day, all left for home except Fr. Lasuén, and Fr. Fuster and Fr. Arroita, the two who were to be in charge of Mission La Purísima, the building of which had already begun. Fr. Cavaller and Ixtil rode with the priests from Santa Barbara and San Buenaventura, whose missions Fr. Joseph greatly desired to see. He and Ixtil were much impressed by the size and splendor of these two newcomers among the missions. They were treated with great hospitality and shown the plans for future building. These impressed them all the more.

"They have to be that way, Ixtil," Fr. Joseph explained as they headed back north. "These missions are much more populous and richer than our little countrified San Luis Obispo."

Ixtil smiled. "Are you explaining this to me or to yourself?"

"You rascal! I suppose mostly for myself." Fr. Joseph laughed. "Honestly, though, the bustle and the crowds we've just seen would wear me out in no time. Let them prosper. But give me the peaceful life, with time to think my own thoughts and pray my own prayers."

"Except for an occasional visit to sharpen you, perhaps?"

Fr. Joseph laughed again. "You know me too well, Ixtil."

Exposure to the great channel missions put ideas into Ixtil's head for improving Mission San Luis Obispo. Moreover, he had witnessed an amazing work by an old carpenter, named Ignacio Vicente Vallejo. Confessing to Ixtil later that he had jumped ship from the Mexican brig *San Andreas* at San Diego a year before, he had come plodding up El Camino one day in the year belonging to God, 1786, and asked Ixtil for a drink of water. While he drank, Ixtil surveyed the large pack he was carrying.

Seeing Ixtil's eyes wander to the pack, its owner had poked it with a grimy thumb. "Tools," he said. "Ever see steel tools?"

"A few."

"Well, *mi pobrecito,* I am a carpenter, and because I know how to use these tools I'm worth *una perla grande* to this mission."

"Probably you are, *Señor*," Ixtil agreed. "We need many carpenter works here. May I call the priest to talk with you?"

The stranger surveyed the mission, not missing the fields around it and the hills around them. "Nice quiet place," Ixtil heard him mutter to himself. "Not too much work. Plenty of food in good years. In bad years we all starve anyways." Aloud he said, *"Muy bien, chiquito.* Call the priest."

That was how Vallejo started being worth *perlas grandes* to Mission San Luis Obispo.

During the winter rains the old man looked at the three streams and their flow of water from time to time. Finally he told Fr. Joseph, "You don't get the water that's coming to you from those streams, Father. Too much brush, too many marshes, too much going around curves which drink up the water. I'll build you an aqueduct, starting up there at the source of Rio San Luis and coming down to the church with a flow that is clean and plentiful."

They discussed what an aqueduct would require, and it was much, but the need for more and better water, whose lack plagued every mission in the province, won out easily.

"From the point of view of an engineer like myself," observed Vallejo, without undue modesty, "the problem is to find a big pool or cataract high up where the stream descends from the hills. Then to lead it along a waterproof channel of boards, always downwards to where it is wanted—namely, down the gullets of thirsty ones at the mission. So first we find the right pool, then the boards from which the water cannot escape as it travels."

One day sufficed for Ixtil and Vallejo to discover a full, deep pool at a sufficient elevation. But months of days went by while crews felled trees large enough and sliced them into boards, and more months and many loads of tar to render them watertight. It was lucky that Ixtil knew, from the building of canoes, the secret places where sticky pitch bubbled out of the earth. Indeed, the whole operation resembled the building of the Chumash canoes. Before it was all over, Ixtil had enlisted the aid of professionals from the seacoast villages.

Nearly a year from its inception, the aqueduct at last reached the mission patio and, to the accompaniment of cheers and dances, the first stream of water flowed into a large barrel, provided for the purpose. Everyone who crossed the quadrangle drank from this barrel. In all except the driest months of summer, the flow was great enough not only to satisfy thirst but also to irrigate the fields nearest the church. The aqueduct became a sight which *Indios* from afar came to admire, and *La Perla Grande* devoted most of his time to conducting tours along it. To get him back for even the simplest carpentry around the mission required a major effort.

The comic little Vallejo lived only six years to enjoy the acclaim so widely accorded him. His achievement, however, made a great impression upon Ixtil and brought visions of other marvelous inventions to benefit his people. Consequently, when a transient Chumash, named Fene, from Mission San Gabriel, stopped overnight at Mission San Luis Obispo with tales of new wonders in the south, Ixtil questioned him closely about them and then took him to Fr. Joseph.

"It is true what I say, *Padre,*" insisted Fene, who seemed to think that his reports were under attack. "At my mission we have now a stonemason, a carpenter, a blacksmith, and a weaver. The stonemason is teaching us how to build thick walls of stones and *adobe* for a big, big church. The weaver, Antonio Domingo Henriquez and his wife Marta make in our sight spinning wheels, warping-frame looms, and all the tools of his craft. He shows our women how to weave every sort of blanket and also cloth for wearing, both wool and cotton. They tell us that the missions farther south have skilled craftsmen like themselves, besides other sorts of workers, all sent from Mexico by the authorities, who pay them to come here to teach us their trades. By the bones of Santiago, *Padre,* it is as I say."

Fr. Joseph thanked him and sent him to get his evening meal from the communal kitchen.

"We must get our share of these teachers, Ixtil, especially to build the church I have had dreams about," the priest said.

"And the weaving, Father!" exclaimed Ixtil. "Ysaga would like to learn that, and many of the other women too. She is always saying that we men are shameless in what we don't wear. Father, this is an opportunity greater than any since the little Vallejo. Let me ride to the missions as far south as San Buenaventura. I will come back with half a dozen of these men, if you will let me have six or seven mules. Perhaps ten would be necessary if there are women also and equipment. Would you lend me ten?"

The priest smiled. "Thanks to *el Dios bueno* for an enthusiastic *alcalde* like you. You shall have the ten mules, plus one for yourself, of course. And one or two other men who speak Spanish persuasively."

"We will leave in the morning early, *Padre.*"

Ixtil traveled south with two assistants and a train of a dozen mules. It turned out that all the artisans who had been sent to California had their families with them, and a few household goods besides. He also found that he could not simply ride into other missions and steal or borrow their instructors. Missions did not steal from one another. His best method proved to be the interception of the artisans while they were on the move from one place to another or just after they had entered California by the land routes or by ship, so that they had not yet settled themselves. None of the artisans, Ixtil learned, was assigned to any specific mission. They were to go where they were most needed.

After learning about this indefiniteness, Ixtil sent one of his companions with all speed back to Fr. Joseph with an urgent request for more mules—at least six, if possible. They came with much slowness, but come at last they did. Eventually, Ixtil was able to ride elatedly into the Mission San Luis compound with a stone-mason, a blacksmith, a maker of shoes, a tailor, two carpenters, and the desirable weaver, Henriquez. Every mule carried a man or a woman or children and some equipment proper to a trade.

Nor had Fr. Joseph been idle during the interval of waiting. He had supervised the erection of several large huts with fireplaces and tile roofs, the repair of others, and the partition of one of the granaries into apartments. The newly arriving families dispersed themselves into these quarters with few problems. Ixtil asked each artisan for a description of the shop he needed for the exercise of his art, which could not be built before it was known what type of craftsman he would catch. Fr. Joseph and Ixtil, in consultation with the craftsmen, decided how many existing shops could be used as they were, or adapted to special needs, and how many additional ones should be constructed outside the stockade.

With most of the mission's labor force assigned to the building, the shops came into existence within about a week and the appropriate furnishings were installed. Shortly thereafter, the various skilled workers began demonstrating their skills. Ixtil saw to it that all his people were given time off from their usual labors to spend some hours each day watching the newcomers at work.

Most of the watchers developed a particular interest in one or another of the crafts being demonstrated, and returned to observe it day after day. Predictably, others showed no enthusiasm for anything new and wandered back to their accustomed work. But to each of those who were interested Ixtil gave the chance to specify one or even two trades in which he would like to receive training. On this basis, he formed classes for instruction, first for an hour a day, then for two hours daily for those who showed greatest promise.

The old work schedules and the new training sessions required some juggling, but slowly everything fell into a regular routine. Life at the mission acquired a new and pleasing variety. The place became a Christ-centered, self-sustaining society, having less and less dependence upon the outside world.

Ixtil would have liked to acquire skill in all the occupations, to watch every demonstration, to become a member of every class of learners, but the new complexity of things also showed itself in his work as *alcalde.* He had to function not merely with the community of Chumash and soldiers and priests but also in addition, with an added layer of highly trained workmen unlike any of the others.

Baffled, Ixtil asked Fr. Joseph one day, "What shall I do with the skilled artisans, Father?"

"What do you mean, 'do with them'?"

"Well, suppose there is a dispute, or even a crime, between one of them and one of my people? Or between one of them and a soldier? Do I judge it on my own or refer it to you?"

"Yes, I see," said the priest, reflecting. "As a general rule, treat matters of *Indios,* soldiers, and priests just as before these newcomers came, judging the same types of offenses as you would have judged then, referring to me, as before, the matters you have always referred. As for the artisans, treat them as citizens on the same level as the *Indios,* and in the same ways."

"But I myself am an *Indio* to the artisans."

"You are an *alcalde,* duly elected. Next year the artisans will have a vote. Meantime they must accept the situation as they find it."

Ixtil was about to continue his objections, but the look of exhaustion, even illness, which was beginning to thin the priest's face stopped him.

"I would like the building of the church to begin soon, Ixtil. This is a Christian mission. The composition of our society is less important than its holiness. I would like to live to see the church completed."

"Yes, Father," said Ixtil with quick love. "We must start laying out its dimensions tomorrow morning after breakfast."

Ixtil relayed the order to the master and apprentice stonemasons, augmented by as many of the mission's general labor force as could be spared from their occupations. By Christmastime the dimensions of a big church, long but rather narrow, had been stepped off and markers planted to show their boundaries, and the deep and wide trench along the outside boundaries had been dug to the depth of a man's height and the width of a man's extended arms. In this trench the masons laid a mighty foundation of stones, chosen for their size and hardness, mixed with mortar, and permitted to dry in place thoroughly. And on this foundation the walls were rising, three feet thick and already taller than a man, with a door in the middle of each side, and at the south end.

Fr. Joseph, who had been practically living in this structure since the first earth was turned, decided that the first Christmas Eve Mass should be said in it. He erected a temporary altar at its north end, thatched it over with brushwood in case of rain. Fortunately, God did not send his rain that Christmas Eve. All the *Indios* of the mission stood shoulder to shoulder in the church's ample confines, responding to the sacred words and eating the body of Christ, while the stars shone bravely overhead and the unfinished walls gave promise of such a church as few of them had seen.

Even without rain that evening, the people stood on a muddy floor. Taking thought for a remedy, Ixtil remembered a hillside near Nipomo where a yellowish sandstone lined the sides through which El Camino ran. If there was enough of it to floor the new church and if he could bring back that quantity in *caretas* to Tixlini, it would furnish not only dry standing but much beauty.

Ixtil drove a *careta* to the hillside, all thirty miles of the distance, and from it cut a large, experimental square. He found that the soft rock quarried easily, without crumbling, to a depth of about ten feet in most places on both sides of El Camino. But could it stand the rough trip to San Luis Obispo by *careta?* He levered the big square into the cart and, driving homeward slowly, with due care for the bumps and hollows in the roadway, proved to himself that the journey could be made that way.

The mission owned many *caretas* to bring in the harvests of the agriculture, but these could not be spared. So Ixtil set the two carpenters to work building a dozen more of great strength. When they were completed, he borrowed from the mission herds a dozen oxen to pull them. Finally, on a morning of early spring, he set out for Nipomo with drivers, a crew of strong men, and tools for quarrying and lifting. They made three trips before the piles of yellow squares, waiting for use in the church flooring, stood high enough outside each door.

When the building's walls reached the required twenty-foot height and the builders moved into the woods to find and cut the roof timbers, long and strong enough to reach across the narrow emptiness between the walls, Ixtil and his crew started laying the floor. Each square had to be cut carefully and smoothed so as to fit snugly among its neighbor squares. This took some doing, but swiftly it was done. By the time the first roof timbers began arriving, several weeks later, the finished floor lay smooth and handsome.

Chapter 17

So spring passed into summer of the year belonging to God, 1789, and it looked as if the main structure of the church would soon be finished. But *el Dios bueno* stretched out His hand and stayed the proud project.

He did so in this manner. A seaman, Aldo Moreno, having jumped ship near Morro Bay during the night's blackness, swam ashore and headed inland toward the mission which he had heard existed up the valley. Thinking to wait until his ship had departed, he joined a wandering Chumash family that was camped in the hills beside *La Perla's* aqueduct. They were hunting deer and picking the ripening blackberries.

In these labors, however, Aldo Moreno took no part, not because he was unwilling but because he was too weak. At first, he thought he had caught a severe fever by the icy swim from the ship, but soon he had reason to believe that he had contracted the cholera which had felled many of his fellows on the ship he had left. He found himself racked by stomach cramps, which he hoped would be relieved by the constant vomiting and equally constant liquid movements which he passed so often in the bushes near the camp that they stank. Also, he thirsted all the time and dragged himself to the aqueduct, as often as he had strength for it, to drink great gulps of the cooling water. On more than one occasion he vomited into the water even while he was drinking it.

All these evil signs frightened the Chumash family. On the second night after Aldo's arrival, they stole away from him in the dark. He heard them go and shouted desperately at them to take him with them. But in the morning he was alone. Although he had no food, he had plenty of water in the aqueduct, which he was sure must go down to the mission. He dragged himself along it, but reaching up to drink became harder and harder. Finally he climbed into the aqueduct, lay down in the water, became delirious, and died. His body was not discovered until the aqueduct inspector, making his regular biweekly trip of inspection, discovered it, and ran to the mission to tell Ixtil. After one horrified glance and a curt word to the inspector to bury the body well away from the aqueduct, Ixtil ran back to forbid any drinking from the barrel in the patio.

But Aldo's sickness had been running into the barrel for several days and had been drunk by many who lived in the rooms surrounding the courtyard, as well as by those from the Chumash village who had any occasion to cross it. Mission San Luis Obispo soon had a full-scale cholera epidemic, though nobody knew its name or any way of treating it. Sufferers overflowed from the hospital into neighboring buildings. Fr. Joseph and Ixtil made a despairing search of *La Medicina Domestica,* without avail.

Ixtil threw the book aside in disgust. "It has to be the bad water, somehow, that the sickness comes from. Let us organize the people to drink from the other streams."

"Few have not already drunk from the water of the aqueduct," Fr. Joseph reminded him.

"But some not as much as others, and some not at all."

"Perhaps, then, even those who drank will not be

equally sick."

"I hope so, Father," said Ixtil. "That is my hope, my prayer."

The priest turned out to be right—tragically right so far as Ixtil's family was concerned. Ixtil and Fr. Joseph contracted only light cases, but Ysaga had stopped by the barrel to talk with some of her friends and the talk had been long and thirsty. And Ysaga had remembered to take home a bucketful for family drinking.

Whatever the reason, she and the three children came down with cases as bad as they could be. Ponce and Juan were especially sick. They would not benefit by being crowded into the hospital, Ixtil thought. Being only slightly ill himself, he was able to nurse all his family, and he brought many pails of water from the safe streams. He spent his days and nights in sponging and cleansing the sick bodies, cooking broth to nourish them if their stomachs would keep it down, rocking the children to sleep in his arms, holding Ysaga close to comfort her in her delirium, and soaking and boiling their clothes with soap root. And he prayed whenever he could remember to.

"Prayers move God," Ixtil had often heard Fr. Joseph say. He prayed with all his soul that *el Dios bueno* would take him instead of his family. One night, he thought he noticed some improvement in Chiquita, but her brothers and her mother grew steadily worse. That night he ran to find Fr. Joseph.

The priest was just recovering from his own siege of the deadly sickness, but he came. In Ixtil's house, he sank to his knees by Ysaga's side, then by the side of each child. Long and passionately the Father prayed and Ixtil with him, holding Ysaga in his arms. Fr. Joseph anointed them all with the holy oils, and the hours ran on.

Ixtil scarcely knew when her breathing stopped, when Ysaga's heart no longer thudded against his own. He was dimly aware that the good priest was trying gently to disengage her body from his clasp. Ixtil resisted automatically.

"She is dead, my friend," Fr. Joseph told him resignedly. "Let me lay her out properly."

Ixtil surrendered her. "And the others?" he demanded, dreading the answer.

"Only Chiquita still lives. She will grow well again, I think."

"Ysaga! Ysaga!" Ixtil cried. "How can I live without you, and our two boys you have taken with you?" All the world was empty. No reply came. He cried again, "Ysaga! Ysaga!" and wept.

He was conscious of Fr. Joseph putting Chiquita into his arms.

"God has left you this little one, Ixtil," the priest said. "She will need you."

"But He has taken three. Werowance was right! This is an evil world—Sup's world." Ixtil's weeping now had anger in it.

Fr. Joseph shook his head. "God's arithmetic is not ours, Ixtil. Life is still to be lived, and heaven's still worth winning."

Ixtil looked down at the face of the little girl, smiling as she slept, which calmed him.

"Father," he said, "I will take the others to the *campo santo* in the morning for burial."

"And I will say a requiem Mass for them and all the others who have died during the night."

El Dios bueno willed that His mission should not perish by reason of the cholera. The three deahs in Ixtil's family were not typical of the mortality suffered by other families and by the yet unmarried men and women resident at San Luis Obispo. Many experienced only slight attacks of the disease and recovered soon. Others, who did not drink the infected water in the patio, did not catch it at all. The *campo santo* was not filled, though its tenanted area increased too much.

Consequently, the gathering of timbers for the church roof ceased only for a week or two. At first, Ixtil could not help in the work. He seemed to be living in a vast silence, in which he would never hear Ysaga's voice again. Scarcely any sounds of the life around him penetrated the silence, except Chiquita's chatter and the doings of the family next door. Ixtil stayed alone with the child in his vacant house, brooding. But then came the evening when Fr. Joseph stood at the door-way.

"You've grieved long enough, Ixtil," the priest said sharply. "This is un-Christian. Ysaga and the boys are safe in heaven, where Our Lord *Jesu* wipes the tears from their eyes. Exert yourself! Work at something!"

"I am still very lonely, Father, and unable to hear the sounds of the world," Ixtil pleaded.

Fr. Joseph rejected the plea with a shake of his head. "The only man who is truly lonely is the one who forgets God. He never forgets you, Ixtil. Do not turn away from Him, as you are doing now. Despite all seemings, He never has turned away from you. But He expects both your love and your obedience. Pray to Him while you work. But work!"

At dawn next morning, Ixtil bestirred himself. Without haste he took from his hut, piece by piece, every object that could be moved. And lastly Chiquita, only half awake on her sleeping mat. When all had been removed, he planted fire on the hut's floor, walls, and roof. From a distance, he and his daughter watched it burn to the ground. She looked at him questioningly but asked no questions.

Then he began to build a new dwelling of tules not
far from the ashes of the old. In this he had much
silent help from his neighbors. When the construction
was finished, they moved the useful objects preserved
from the old hut into the new one. As a token of his
gratitude, Ixtil gave them much of the food he had
saved. He thanked them also with heartfelt words.

Early next morning, having fed Chiquita and himself, Ixtil asked whether she would like to come along
and watch him work that day. She looked at him
gravely and asked, "Are you men still building the
church?"

On being assured that they were, she smiled enchant-
ingly and said, "Then of course I must go with you.
Mommy used to, sometimes, and left me lonely. Now
that she has gone away I must do all the things she
used to do, like coming with you."

Ixtil forced an answering smile. "Naturally, " he
replied.

"Will we get home in time for me to do the sweeping and the cooking, the way she did?"

Ixtil nodded. "But first you and I must choose our
lunch to take with us, Chica."

While he took down several strips of dried deer
meat, hanging under the hut's smoke hole, Chiquita
collected two handfuls of grapes which had been transformed to raisins by the sun. These and Ixtil's meat,
and a bit of chocolate, went into the carrying basket
she slung across her shoulder.

Arrived at the church, with the child walking de-
murely at his side, Ixtil saw that a number of straight
tree trunks about thirty feet long lay in orderly rows
along the rising walls. Cut in the eastern hills, he
knew, and dragged by mule teams to the mission. Men
were sawing them to identical lengths; others, with ax,
adze, and sledge hammer, were changing their round-

ness to squareness all along their length.

It was a great work, requiring thousands of cuts. But for the first time since Ysaga died, Ixtil felt the blood singing through his body as he worked, and his gloom lifting. He was glad the work was long and worthy of his strength.

He had kept a watchful eye on Chiquita all morning as she played nearby on a pile of rocks that had been gathered for the church's walls. When the mission bell struck the signal for food and rest, he joined her. Proudly, while they ate together, she showed him a small house she was making out of slivers of rock. It had walls and a sloping roof and a doorway in one wall. Inside, if you looked through the door with your cheek on the ground, you could see a tiny stone altar. In fact, it looked a good deal like the mission church.

"Of course, it's not finished yet," she apologized.

"No?" asked Ixtil. "What is lacking?"

It turned out that she had plans for doors and windows, and even statues of Mary and the saints. "Probably better than the big ones we are carving," Ixtil declared, hugging her. He was telling her about Our Lady of Guadalupe when the bell signaled a return to labor.

As the big church progressed, its carpenters decided they must have at least another half dozen of the long tree trunks for rafters to cross from one wall to the other along the whole length of the building; so Ixtil went with the others into the forests. And, of course, Chiquita came along, walking beside him in the smooth places, riding on his shoulders in the rough places.

The party had to search a long time before finding and marking the six long, straight trunks they needed. Next came the felling. Next the trimming off of all side branches. Next, and hardest, the transporting.

The other woodcutters simply camped wherever darkness found them. Every evening, however, Ixtil carried Chiquita back to the mission to be properly fed and looked after. And every morning they returned to the camps in the forest.

The more trouble he took for her, the dearer she became: an unfailing source of cheer in a bleak world. And not for him only. Six-year-old Chiquita, with her ready, gap-toothed smile, also became the darling of the woodcutters. Through her, Ixtil came really to know them to their depths and to feel for them an affection stronger than mere liking. Reciprocating, they befriended him in return.

She has restored me to life, the blessed little one, reflected Ixtil gratefully. God can still be good. These discoveries healed his wounds.

When at last the additional tree trunks lay along the church walls, Ixtil and his fellow woodcutters turned back into carpenters, reducing round trees to square-cut rafters. Fr. Joseph seemed to spend all his time watching them.

One day he remarked to Ixtil, "You look strongly alive. The physical labor in the open air has been very good for you. And of course your little imp, Chiquita—she wins all hearts."

Leaning on his ax, Ixtil scanned the priest's face. "I wish I could say the same about you, Father, but it is not so. You look like a man who should be in bed. Can't you let us finish the church, without worry? Standing always in these November winds is not good for you."

The priest looked keenly at Ixtil for a moment, then looked away. "These breezes have nothing to do with it. My heart does not function well, I think. The other evening it gave great pain in the chest and along the left arm. But that has passed and I am well again."

"Lend me the *Medicina Domestica,* Father."

"I have searched it, Ixtil."

"Nevertheless, please let me borrow it. Your life does not belong to you, dear Father, but, after God, to the whole mission." He might have added "especially me," but did not.

"If God permits, I should like to live until this church is finished and in use, or at least through this Christmas," said Fr. Joseph wistfully.

But God permitted neither.

November gave way to December. For several days the priest did not come to watch his church grow under the workers' hands. One evening after dinner, Ixtil took Chiquita to the priests' house to see Fr. Joseph. Informed of Fr. Cavaller's illness, *Padre Presidente* Lasuén had sent Fr. Miguel Pieras and Fr. Miguel Giribet to take over his work at the mission. It was Fr. Pieras who opened the door at Ixtil's knock.

"Fr. Joseph is not seeing any visitors, Ixtil," he said.

"I am not a visitor, Father, but, since the mission began seventeen years ago, I venture to say, his friend, his disciple, his *alcalde,* indebted to him in all things. I beg you, tell him at least that I am here."

Fr. Pieras smiled warmly. "I know a little about your past together. I will tell him." He returned almost immediately. "He asks you to come in."

Ixtil found Fr. Joseph in bed, breathing short, quick breaths. He reached out a hand, which Ixtil, kneeling, took between both of his. "It is good of you to come, my son, *mi hijo,* not of the flesh but of the spirit."

"How goes it, *Padre?"* asked Ixtil, anxiously scanning the wise, worn face, so pale.

"Not well. I am an old man. My heart tells me *very* old."

"Forty-nine years only. Barely middle age. But it's true, you have always worked harder than anybody else. No wonder you are weary."

"Unto death," the priest whispered.

Panic struck into Ixtil. "No. You cannot die. What would I do without you? I am a selfish man. I need you."

"What will you do? Why, live on as a loving father to little Chiquita. Also, as a just and merciful *alcalde,* leading your people, teaching them to be good Christians, good citizens, in the years to come."

He paused for breath. "But you have one fault, my son. When you are hurt, you strike at God, Who loves you. Through all the apparent tragedies of life, hold fast to the knowledge that He loves you and is guiding you in ways that only He knows."

"Must it be good-bye now?"

"Never! Between two good Christians there can be no good-bye, but only *hasta la vista*—in heaven."

Ixtil knelt weeping by the bedside, holding desperately to the offered hand, until Fr. Pieras came to lead him away.

In the morning, this kindly priest came to tell Ixtil that Fr. Joseph Cavaller died during the night.

The grief was great but not prostrating for Ixtil. Fr. Joseph's reminder about the farewell of good Christians had struck deep. As he ate the breakfast Chica had cooked for him, he became aware that he had a duty to tell his people the news of Fr. Joseph's death, and to comfort them, as nearly as possible, as the Father would have done. So he and Chiquita visited house after house all through the village.

He found the people, most of them, badly shocked by the mortality of the only priest who had served them continually since the mission's first foundation. They were so sad that Chica felt their sadness and started crying, too. To family after family, huddling together as if for comfort when the news spread, and finally to the crowd that stood silently outside the priests' house, Ixtil told the excellent manner of Fr. Joseph's Christian death.

Although priests differ in physical body and personal character, he assured them, they all receive from *el Dios bueno* the power of turning the bread and wine into the body and blood of Jesus at the altar. Fr. Pieras and Fr. Giribet also had that power. Moreover, they were just and kind men. Also, they well understood both the medicine and the agriculture.

He ended by leading the people in singing the "Alabado," that compact profession of praise, as Fr. Serra had called it. Then he dismissed them to their homes, for who could work on such a day? Ixtil himself was unable to keep his mind on anything but the loss of Fr. Joseph.

As the crowd dispersed, Fr. Pieras came out of the priests' house to tell Ixtil that he had sent swift messengers on horseback to Missions Purisima, Santa Barbara, San Antonio, and San Carlos to invite their priests to attend the requiem Mass and the subsequent burial. For what day and hour, he asked, should they schedule it so as to be sure that all those priests who came would be in time for the Mass?

Ixtil pondered. "By tomorrow night at earliest, I think, depending on many factors."

"Suppose, then, we set the Mass for noon, day after tomorrow?"

"That would be wise, Father. May I instruct the carpenters to start making the coffin?"

"Yes. A good thought."

Fr. Joseph's body was lying in his box when a priest from La Purisima and one from Santa Barbara rode in together during the morrow's night. The next morning brought Fr. Sitjar from San Antonio, accompanied by *Padre Presidente* Lasuén, who had been visiting there, thanks to the Providence of God.

"Where should the body be buried, Father?" Ixtil asked Fr. Pieras. "Assuredly not in the *campo santo,* which is already crowded and lacking in dignity for a priest?"

Fr. Pieras smiled. "You know, Ixtil, I think that is where Joseph would prefer to be. But for edification we will put him under the church floor, near the altar, where he can hear the Masses being sung and smell the incense—until his resurrection."

"Can his body really hear and smell?"

"Only after a manner of speaking. But truly it is holy to be laid to one's rest near an altar. The other California missions are already doing this for their priests. In Spain, great nobles contend for tombs near the most sacred place in every church."

Ixtil nodded. "We Chumash feel the same. We will be happy for the sake of Fr. Joseph, whom we love. I am glad we brought the lovely sandstone from Nipomo. It will cover him well."

At the appointed hour the requiem Mass was concelebrated by the six priests in embroidered vestments while *Indios* from miles around stood inside and outside, hearing and seeing what they could. After the *Ite, Missa est,* it was a simple matter to carry the coffin from where it lay before the altar to the waiting grave, from which the sandstone slab had been removed, to lower it gently, and to fit the flooring back over it.

Ixtil saw it all, and had the opportunity to say his farewell again to the holy priest who had educated him and guided his ways. Afterward, outside the church he drew deep breaths of ocean-scented air. He had had more than enough of death, and felt a guilty sense of relief. He needed solitude. Above the unfinished church towered San Luis peak, smoothly rounded, green with growth from the early rains.

"I will lift up mine eyes to the hills, from whence my strength comes," he remembered, and suddenly wanted to climb the peak. Taking Chiquita on his shoulders, he started to climb upward, step after step, enjoying the play of his muscles, the air in his panting lungs, until he sank to rest on the grass near the summit.

What and where was his life to be, now that he had lost almost his whole family and, besides, Fr. Joseph, the shepherd of his soul?

Miles away to the northwest shone the sea off Morro; to the west, just as far, the sea of San Luis Bay. Not on those glittering surfaces, nor on the heights where he now lay, could he serve the holy priests who served others. His place was in the valley at his feet, where his people lived out their ordinary lives, needing whatever help an ordinary Ixtil could give them from time to time. And beginning to rise in their midst stood the church, which would offer through the years a kind of aid not to be given by any man.

Chiquita, nestled against his shoulder, looked up at him with her gap-toothed smile.

It was enough.